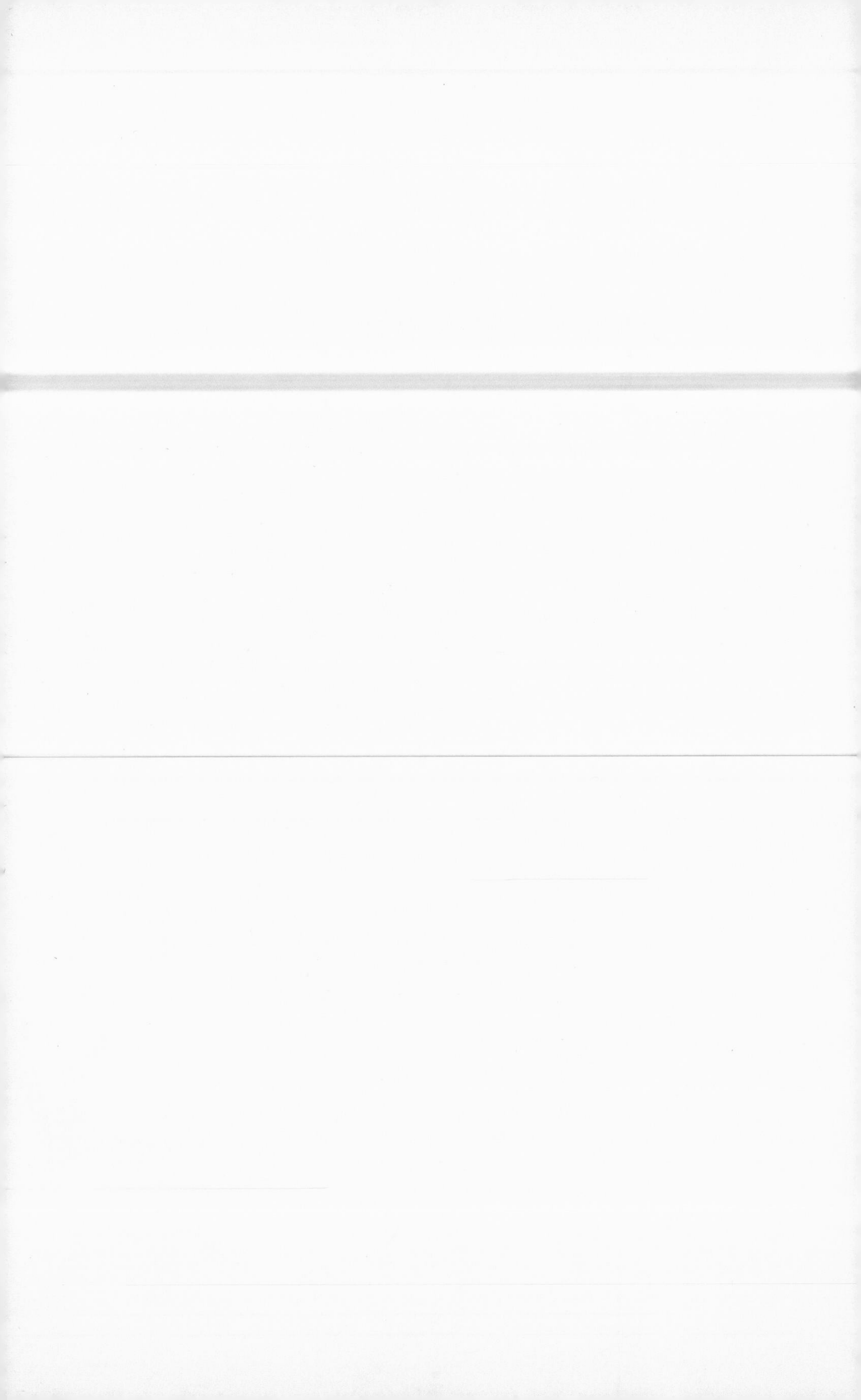

CHASING
TIGER

OTHER BOOKS BY CURT SAMPSON

Texas Golf Legends

The Eternal Summer: Palmer, Hogan, and Nicklaus in 1960, Golf's Golden Year

Full Court Pressure

Hogan

The Masters

Royal and Ancient

Five Fundamentals (with Steve Elkington)

CHASING TIGER

CURT SAMPSON

ATRIA BOOKS
New York London Toronto Sydney Singapore

For information address Atria Books, 1230 Avenue
of the Americas, New York, NY 10020

ISBN: 0-7434-4212-1

First Atria Books hardcover printing June 2002

10 9 8 7 6 5 4 3 2 1

For information regarding special discounts for bulk purchases,
please contact Simon & Schuster Special Sales at 1-800-456-6798 or
business@simonandschuster.com

Designed by Jaime Putorti

Printed in the U.S.A.

In memory of two great guys,
Art Wall and
Earl Elliott

ACKNOWLEDGMENTS

Special thanks to:

Bill Earley

Bob and Ann Sampson

John Strawn

Michael D'Antonio

David McCormick, agent

Judith Curr, publisher

Luke Dempsey, editor

And to:

PGA Tour: Mark Calcavecchia, Brandel Chamblee, Ben Curtis, Clark Dennis, Henry Hughes, Charles Howell III, David Moreland IV, Brad Faxon, Tom Lehman, Andrew Magee, Vaughn Moise, Curtis Strange

PGA of America: Bob Denney, Bill Eschenbrenner, David Leadbetter, Julius Mason, Mike Morrow, Herb Page, Dan Strimple, Tad Weeks

Media: Jim Apfelbaum, Adam Barr, Ron Balicki, Ward Clayton, John Feinstein, John Garrity, Pete Freeman, Kaye

Kessler, Peter Kessler, Carl Mickelson, Pete McDaniel, Marino Paracenzo, Tim Rosaforte, Bruce Selcraig, Guy Yocom, John Ziegler

Research: Morgan Ordway

Augusta: Danny and Nicole Fitzgerald, Sid Gates, Charlie and Deborah Howell, Jerry Matheis, Kathy Starrett

Columbus: Bill Case, who also helped a lot on a previous book, *Royal and Ancient*

Cleveland: Alastair J. Johnston, Mark H.McCormack

Dallas: Rocky Hambric, Ann Quinn Staton, Nita Wiggins

Ennis: Clay and John Sampson

Houston: Jack Burke, Jr., Burt Darden, Brooke and Connie Farnsworth, Debbie Zeringue

New York: Carol Costello, Megan Kent

Tulsa: Tona Coleman, Bob and Kim Jandebeur, Gaylen Groce, Barbara Sessions, Mark Snow

San Antonio: Jack and Nancy Harden

CONTENTS

CHASING TIGER

INTRODUCTION

He haunts the muni courses and driving ranges of Austin, Texas, a slim black man of perhaps thirty, and his routine never varies. He always parks in a remote corner of the lot, perhaps because his car, an old Datsun, strikes the only false note in his portrayal. He withdraws a giant, professional-looking golf bag from the trunk, hoists it to his shoulder, and walks toward the clubhouse like a visiting king. His demeanor is serious, fiercely so, which makes it easier for him to pretend he doesn't see the double takes he inspires, and must secretly love.

Does he own another outfit? No one has ever seen him wearing any pants but black, any shirt but red, or any logo but Nike's checkmark. He'll spend hours putting at Jimmy

Clay Municipal Golf Club, so many hours that the staff and the regulars have stopped noticing. “I’d kind of like to know what extremes his obsession goes to in his private life,” comments Carl Mickelson, who plays frequently at Jimmy Clay. “But I don’t ask. He gives off this eerie vibe, like he’s been detached from day-to-day life for too long. Nobody talks to him.”

A newcomer can’t help but stare, however, at the clothes, the walk, the look, at the middle finger on his right hand taped *just so,* and especially at his elaborate performance on the putting green. He’ll crouch behind a practice putt as if it were for the Open, his hands cupped on either side of the bill of his hat. While the meaningless putt rolls toward the hole, he lifts the putter up in anticipation, as earnest as if lifting a fluttering battle flag. He salutes successful putts with a clenched right fist, shaken once, emphatically. For the ball that does not fall, a three-part reaction: a sigh, with the head back, often with eyes closed for one long second; a withering stare at the hole; and the pièce de résistance, a completely authentic placing of his hands on his hips.

“Wow, you sure practice a lot,” a stranger says.

“Got to,” he replies. “I’m a pro.”

But he’s not. As at any public course, Jimmy Clay’s pairings are random and perverse, so you never know with whom you might be spending the next few hours. If you’re very unlucky, you get the fake Tiger. He’s got the preshot ritual down pat, of course, and he sets up to the ball in the athletic, butt-out posture of the real thing. But finally, he’s got to hit, and the poor bastard fights a vicious slice with every swing and struggles to break 90. He grinds away like he's in Augusta rather than Austin, as if it's the last day in the Masters and he's a shot behind Duval. He doesn't talk, and he takes forever.

BACK WHEN THE CLEVELAND BROWNS were winning, a friendless kid who lived a couple of doors from my parents in Ohio would take a football out into his front yard on fall afternoons. The little boy would put the ball on the ground and stand above it, his hands ready to receive the snap from the invisible center. Like Bernie Kosar, the beloved Browns quarterback, the only calm man among the eighty-six thousand lunatics in the stadium, the boy would have to raise his hands high, a gesture to calm the multitudes. His head would swivel like Bernie's as he read the defense, and his head would bob as he called out, "Red, thirty-two, thirty-two, hut, hut." And then the friendless kid would fade back to pass to no one.

My mother loved to watch from the kitchen window. "Rob, come look at this," she'd say to my father, and they'd stand there together for a minute, reminded of their own four sons, who danced to similar dreamy music when we were all much younger.

Athletic fantasy courses strongly through a little boy's blood. And as much as any sport, golf provides a canvas on which to paint complicated feelings of identity, admiration, and love. For example, a generation of aspiring golfers in Texas walked between their shots with a limp, a touching homage to Ben Hogan, whose legs had been damaged in a car-bus collision. A decade later Arnie ruled, and any young dreamer could get him down in a day—his slash of a swing, a putting stance in which big toes and knees touched, and cigarettes. The cigarettes needed to be inhaled deeply just before a shot, then flicked sharply to the ground, and they had to be L&M's. Arnie the naturalist gave way in turn to Jack the technician, a complicated and nuanced performer with scores of scientific-seeming quirks to imitate. If you couldn't do Jack's swing, you could try for the sweep of blond hair, the headcovers (knit, with green-and-white pom-poms as big as volleyballs), his clubs, his clothes, the way his eyebrows knit when he was staring down a putt, or his pace of play, which was glacial.

No modern or postmodern player resonated like Hogan, Palmer, or Nicklaus, however. Possibly the best and most exciting athletes in any sport for three successive decades, the three men converged at Cherry Hills in the U.S. Open of 1960, a kind of symbolic torch-passing that confirmed each man's greatness and each man's style. And then tournament golf settled into an epoch of bland high professionalism. In the eighties and nineties, golf and golfers fell from favor while basketball players like the NBA's Bird, Johnson, and Jordan ascended in the popular mind. Some amateurs affected the sleeveless sweaters and insouciance of Fred Couples, or Greg Norman's fire, Johnny Miller's ice, or the wide stance of Curtis Strange. But no one, not even Tom Watson, the best post-Jack performer, really rang the bell. Then along came Tiger.

His smile, his style, and the graceful violence of his swing added up to a presentation so attractive that it begged to be imitated—though some, of course, take it too far. Like that young man in Austin, or the woman in the tiger-striped cat suit who creeps through his gallery, muttering to herself like a bag lady. In part because of his look, and in part because of several unique circumstances—cultural, commercial, and historical—Woods may have greater impact on his sport than anyone ever has. In just five years as a pro, he's changed how the game is played, how much a professional might be paid to play, and who aspires to play it. He might even touch the world in some still-undefined way, as a force for Good, perhaps fulfilling his father and mother's staggering prediction for their remarkable son. Deacon Palmer and Charlie Nicklaus certainly never compared their baby boys to Gandhi.

But even if Tiger's career stopped tomorrow, and he had no more effect on global affairs than did Dan Quayle, his impact has already shaken the ground.

LET'S REVIEW:

Eldrick Woods was born in a hospital near Los Angeles, not in a manger.

His father had been an athlete in his native Kansas, a baseball player good enough to earn a scholarship to Kansas State. On road trips for the Wildcats, Earl Woods, a catcher and the only man of color on the team and the first black baseball player in the Big Eight Conference, often had to stay in substandard Jim Crow hotels. Earl never forgot or forgave the insult. There was a war on when he graduated from KSU in May 1953. He gravitated to the military, possibly because it was, following President Truman's orders to desegregate the armed forces, the least color-conscious institution in America. But again Woods encountered racism, and he hoarded the bitter memories like coins in a piggy bank. He married a woman named Barbara and started a family that he didn't see much. Another war came. He trained to become a Green Beret—"the only organization that treats you at face value," he said—and twice volunteered for combat duty in Vietnam. On a third and final assignment in Southeast Asia, he met a tiny Thai woman, Kultida Punsawad, then working as a receptionist in an office in Bangkok. Earl returned to the States, divorced Barbara, and sent for Tida. They married in New York in 1973, his second marriage, her first, and settled in Southern California.

Earl had married up. The Punsawads had money—Tida's daddy owned a tin mine and the family owned a fleet of city buses in Bangkok. Fair of face and full of grace, Tida's appeal was obvious. Earl had some charm, too.

Their son, Eldrick Tiger, born December 30, 1975, would be their only child, the biggest project of their lives, and the main thing holding them together.

Their union joined at least five races and two religions. Tida was Thai, Chinese, Caucasian, and Buddhist. Earl blended black, white, Shawnee, Chinese, and the kind of Christianity that allowed him to talk with his dead sisters.

Earl recalls giving his new bride a speech about American racism soon after she arrived. He quotes himself in the second of his three books about Tiger, *Playing Through*. "In the United States, there are only two colors, white and nonwhite," he says he told his bride. "So don't think you can ever be a full-fledged citizen here." What he taught his son about race must have been similar, but rougher, more blunt, and directed to a goal. It's the same speech thousands of weary black parents have given their kids: You know what these people think you are. You can't settle for being as good as them. You've got to be better.

Earl worked as a buyer for defense contractor McDonnell Douglas, a logical career choice for a former Army man. Less logical, perhaps, was the location of Earl and Tida's first house, in Cypress, California. "We broke the color barrier in our neighborhood," Tiger would recall. "We were the first and only for many years . . . I always felt like an outsider."

But that feeling didn't only come from vile racism. For like little Wolfie Mozart, who composed a pretty good minuet at age five and a full symphony at age eight, Tiger knew he was different in a most positive way. Though separated by two centuries and an ocean, the two prodigies led similar early lives. Both fathers recognized and cultivated their sons' genius; each, in fact, would build his own life around nourishing his child's gift. When Wolfgang was eight, he and his father, Leopold—like Earl Woods, not a rich man—left their home in Salzburg, Austria, and traveled hard for three years. The kid performed, and his father or his mother, Anna Maria, collected fees and arranged meals, transportation, and lodging. Fans and supporters often put them up, just as they would for Earl or Tida and Tiger in junior golf tournaments. Wolfie, who wrote notes before he could write words, had a dog named Bimperl. Little Tiger won his first competition at age three and a half and called his dog Boom Boom. Both children lived to practice.

Royal families figured in both lives. The father with a powdered wig acquired patrons in Empress Maria Theresa and Emperor Francis. The father with plaid golf socks found or was found by International Management Group, the giant sports agency, which put him on the payroll as a "scout," with the tacit understanding that Tiger would not look elsewhere when the time came to select an agent. When the boy wonder from Salzburg grew up, he found himself in vicious competition with other songwriters and musicians, who sniped at him and attempted to undermine their more talented competitor. Wolfgang Amadeus Mozart died at age thirty-six, a morbid, depressed man with an alcohol problem, which is where the parallels with Tiger surely end.

In addition to complexion and a prodigiousness as great in its way as Mozart's, another thing made Eldrick different from the other kids. His mother would not trust his care to anyone else; Tiger never had a baby-sitter. If this degree of indulgence seems foreign, even perverse, "Tiger was raised as an Asian child, not as an American," Earl wrote. "The way Tiger was taught to respect his parents and other adults, to rely on his instincts and feelings, to be unselfish and generous . . . these are all tenets of Asian philosophy and culture." It's hard to miss Earl's superior attitude, or the implied insult to American children and their parents.

But a more important point—as crucial, perhaps, as the father's militarism—is the role in Tiger's life of his mother's Buddhism. Westerners often see Buddhism as mystical and impenetrable, but it's relatively simple and practical. Its founder, Siddhartha Gautama, born 557 years before Christ in what is now borderland between India and Tibet, was a prince who gave away everything at age twenty-nine to live the rest of his days as a homeless ascetic. After six years of study and privation, he found what he'd been looking for—not heaven, not God, not a savior, but enlightenment. How to get to an understanding of the true nature of the world—and thus avoid suffering—is the point of Buddhism. To walk Buddha's path to nirvana requires no worship and no faith, and thus no great intellectual leap. Buddha refused to speculate on what if anything preceded Existence or the look of the face of God or even if God exists. The endless questioning on the ancient Greek model—knowledge for its own sake—he found an utter waste of time. In fact the Buddha listed fourteen questions he wouldn't even entertain, and one of them—Creation—is the linchpin of Christianity.

Tiger is a Christmas tree Buddhist. Half-smiling stone and metal Buddhas sit peacefully here and there throughout his childhood home, coexisting with the Protestant Christianity Earl brought to the house. A little Buddha amulet, a gift from his Thai grandmother, clings to a chain around his neck. While Earl and the Cypress Independent School District taught Eldrick the significance of gift giving in December and of Easter in the spring, Tida and Grandma exposed Tiger to the Eightfold Noble Path. He certainly seems to have incorporated step eight—Right Concentration—into his golf. The Buddhist Instruction Retreat describes this path as being "aloof from the world, from evil, dwelling in solitude, ardent, diligent, resolute one-pointedness of mind through intense meditation and reflection."

Too much can be made of this wisdom from the East theme, however. Sometimes, Tiger's the one making it. "He says he's seeking perfection—which sounds sexy and mysterious—as a person and as a golfer," comments Fran Pirrozola, the mental coach to the New York Yankees and to a dozen or more PGA Tour players. "I think that's to throw the other players off. What he's really got is the focus and calmness to hit perfect golf shots."

While the exact contribution of his spiritual leanings remains an intriguing mystery, the rest of the Woods bio is as familiar as a beer commercial. His father took up golf at age forty-two, just months before Tida gave birth to Tiger. Earl, already hooked, put a golf club in the baby's crib. He pulled Tiger's high chair out into the garage while he pounded balls into a net. Still in Pampers, the kid grabbed a club and . . . Eureka! The little prodigy's appearance on the Mike Douglas TV show at age three is more vivid, for many of us, than anything in our own lives at the same age. The next year Earl hired the best instructors he could find, or could afford, including, importantly, a mental coach. Tiger's golf game bloomed like a hothouse flower. He won the USGA Junior thrice in succession. At age sixteen, he debuted on the PGA Tour, at the Los Angeles Open, and Palmer and Nicklaus predicted greatness for this young man with the terrifying length and the concentration of a chess grand master. In the company of Earl or Tida, he won everything the American Junior Golf Association had to offer. In the midst of this unprecedented success and excitement, he turned eighteen and became the youngest-ever winner of the United States Amateur. A lot of people wondered where he would go to college.

Tiger seriously considered only two schools, Stanford and the University of Nevada at Las Vegas, whose campuses were about the same distance from home. J. T. Higgins, then the assistant coach at UNLV and now the head coach at Texas A&M, remembers the process vividly. "NCAA rules prevented us from talking to him, so we talked to everyone around him," Higgins recalled, "like Jay Brunza, his mental coach, and a doctor—a dermatologist—who was a good friend of the family. You're allowed five campus visits, but Tiger did only two. One of them was to us.

"It was a little unusual. We met for brunch at the president's house. The entire accounting department was there, because he'd said he wanted to major in accounting. Then we went out to Shadow Creek [the extremely high-end golf course belonging to casino owner Steve Wynn] but we couldn't play. NCAA rules. Unless it's a university-owned course, you can't take a recruit to play. So we just rode around and had another great meal.

"It came down to the last night. Tiger called Coach Knight and said he was going to Stanford. Coach Knight was just devastated. I said 'Coach, it's just one player. We'll get someone else.' He said, 'You don't understand. I saw Hogan. I saw Nicklaus. And this is the best golfer I've ever seen in my life.' "

Higgins talked while walking in the gallery of his umpteenth junior golf tournament of the summer, searching for the next Tiger. "But it's funny how it worked out. We got Ted Oh, and we couldn't have gotten both Ted and Tiger, because they didn't get along as junior golfers. Tiger only stayed two years at Stanford. Then we got Jeremy Anderson, and we won the NCAA. We wound up better without Tiger."

The Stanford coach was Wally Goodwin, a gray-haired and ultrasincere former basketball coach whose searching blue eyes bulge with intensity. He knew how to run a fast break and he sure knew how to recruit, having already induced future pros Notah Begay and Casey Martin to enroll at the Harvard of the West. Although the Cardinal won no NCAA championships during his short stay, Tiger won the individual trophy and two more U.S. Amateurs. Within hours—perhaps minutes—after holing out to win his final Amateur, in 1996 at Pumpkin Ridge in Portland, Oregon, Tiger, with a few strokes of his pen, became a professional, a client of IMG, an endorser for Nike, and very wealthy. The Nike deal paid ten million dollars a year. With Tiger gone, national interest in college and amateur golf faded to gray.

But Tiger never left the stage.

Like the shark in *Jaws* or the storm clouds gathering in *The Perfect Storm,* Woods is there even when he's not physically present. He dominates the conversations and preoccupies the minds of a hundred different constituencies, from agents to Zen Buddhists, including but not limited to fans, TV, writers, tabloid newspapers, junior golfers and their parents, equipment manufacturers, golf course architects, tournament officials, eligible women, and corporate

America. His fellow pros in tournament interview rooms start chewing their gum faster when the questions about themselves are perfunctory and few, and then the real point of the exercise begins. "How do you think Tiger's gonna do on these par fives this week?" "Do you think Augusta National is trying to Tiger-proof the course?" Tom Lehman or Phil Mickelson or David Duval take a deep breath and politely say, "Maybe you should ask Tiger," but they can't help but feel diminished that the subject always returns to Woods.

ON THE TOUR, life events competed for attention. J. P. Hayes discovered to his joy that his wife was pregnant. Charles Howell III, the young man who may become Tiger's greatest threat, wondered what his fiancée, Heather, was doing back in Oklahoma. While Howell thought about marriage, Mark Calcavecchia pondered the slow death of divorce, and Brad Faxon, a weary veteran of both, married for the second time.

Up close you can see all the people chasing Tiger, and how infuriatingly hard he is to catch, as if this man who is so real you can smell his breath is also invisible. Snippets from a year in pursuit: "For us, unless Tiger's there, there is no tournament," a reporter from CNN tells you. "He *makes* this tour," says Jeff Burell, Curtis Strange's caddie. "The Tour needs Tiger, but Tiger don't need them." In May, Rich Skyzinski of the USGA traveled to Tulsa and returned full of rue. "Tiger did the Media Day for the U.S. Open by video. He wore a white T-shirt. No, I can't remember any other defending champion who didn't show up. He couldn't have been less interested." Tiger's got valid reasons for being guarded, said Butch Harmon. He gets death threats. He hears the N-word. And though most of the crowd figuratively carries Tiger on its shoulders just as they once lifted Arnold Palmer, "Tiger has a totally different circumstance," Harmon says. "Because in Arnold's day, in the sixties, and even in the seventies, people were different. People had more respect for things and they weren't pushy. In [Tiger's] gallery you see grown men running over the top of little six- and seven-year-olds. It's getting crazy out there."

Perhaps Tiger's seen more clearly from a distance than from up close. If you could climb a mountain and look back at the last century in golf, you'd see two men standing at the head of two lines. The man with the mustache and the pipe is Harry Vardon, the best player of his age and the first to master golf's dramatically new technology. A couple of tinkerers at B. F. Goodrich Tire and Rubber in Akron had invented a new way to build a golf ball, which was a ball within a ball, with a long thin rubber thread wound around and around the little sphere within. Compared to the gutta percha then in use—a solid sphere of tree sap—the Haskell was quicksilver, and the slow-swinging, precise Vardon was its first master.

Byron Nelson, with his forceful, upright swing, was the first to master an equally revolutionary advance in equipment, the steel shaft. Byron stood at the front of the second line. America had applied its industrial genius to golf, inspiring the modern power game that has now reached its peak.

Someday we'll look back from the mountaintop and see that like Harry and Byron, Tiger also started his own line, achieving the perfect match of technique and new equipment. Titanium clubheads as big as canned hams and as forgiving as a grandmother, consistently lively golf balls that don't hook or slice much, and near perfection in shafts and playing surfaces all urged aggression in what was once a subtle game. From Tiger and evermore, grips became stronger, swings harder, and torsos more muscled.

Meanwhile, armies pursue him.

And who is Tiger chasing? Well, that one's easy. His prey is an old man with a cane and a straw hat, standing placid and wise as a saint in the shade of a river birch tree. A few feet away a four-foot umbrella reflector focuses light on two chairs. There's a big camera on a tripod, and a photographer and his assistant futzing with focuses, light meters, backup cameras, and film. Twelve other photographers of lower status wait behind a yellow rope, taking experimental looks at the empty chairs through their viewfinders. The old man pays no heed to the quiet commotion and seems to be enjoying the shade and the smell of spring. He comments about the fine quality of the brickwork on a nearby building. "I remember when they built that," he says. He can talk about masonry, and carpentry, and animal husbandry. He could also tell Tiger a thing or two about psychological dominance, and how a warrior can exist inside a gentle man. But that conversation is for another time.

Woods finally comes over the hill to where the old man has been waiting. Tiger shakes his hand and feels like a kid again, because the old man's mitts are so large and strong they dwarf his own. "Hello, Tiger," the old man says.

"Hello, Mr. Nelson," says Tiger.

1

TOTAL COMMITMENT!

> In my department, there are six people who are afraid of me, and one small secretary who is afraid of all of us. I have one other person working for me who is not afraid of anyone, not even me, and I would fire him quickly, but I'm afraid of him.
>
> —Joseph Heller, *Something Happened*

The chase begins on the practice tee.

It's an agonizing pursuit, because progress is slow, hard to measure, and harder to hold. You might towel off after hitting five hundred balls with the uneasy feeling that you're just another stupid, spinning dog who thinks he's finally gaining on his tail. When you're chasing Tiger, and not just improvement, the goal seems to keep receding into the distance. Because Tiger's practicing too, probably harder and smarter than you are.

So tread softly on the practice tee, and keep your voice down. For the mind of the man at work is like a napping baby in a stuffy room, perched on the thin edge between sweet dreams and cranky wakefulness. Just one mis-hit golf ball and the fretting starts. This could be a trend, baby, his inner voice whispers. You need a lesson, you need a rest, your clubs aren't right. You should have stretched before you came out here. Or did you stretch too much? Maybe your wife should be here. Maybe she should go away. You could be losing it.

He could be losing it, thinks the caddie, calculating 5 percent of the money a man who hits shots like that might win this week. The batmen stand behind their employers with nothing much to do, insecurity and caffeine keeping them upright. Every caddie knows the gentle modern phrase for "you're fired." They've all heard it before: "Joe, you've done a great job. But I think I need a change." Yeah, like a baby needs a new diaper, the dismissed looper thinks but doesn't say. He's afraid to. If he lets it get ugly he'll have a harder time getting another bag to carry.

Perhaps our pro strikes a second bad shot, and a third. Then a calm voice may intrude into his consciousness. "You're sliding under it a bit. Let's just slow it down and get back to thinking about stability, here"—the man with the soothing voice is touching the golfer now, with an intimate hand on a knee or a shoulder or the small of the back—"and here." The instructor speaks softly, for these words are meant for no one else. Another shot goes off line, or flies too low, or too high, or with too little force. The golfer's jaw muscles ripple as he rakes out another golf ball from the pile. And the teacher wonders, did I say the wrong words, or were they the right words poorly expressed? While he'll have a hundred students besides this one, instructors are more sensitive and image conscious than caddies, so for them dismissal by a student is castration. Besides, losing a high-profile client is not good for trade. A really solid shot: "That's it! That's pure. That's Hogan."

Hogan is right. An obsessive man named William Ben Hogan discovered the joy of incessant practice seventy years ago, and as he won U.S. Opens and his influence spread, the headquarters of professional golf gradually moved from the bar to the rehearsal hall. As 1956 Masters and PGA champion Jack Burke likes to say, every golf course had its own sports psychologist back then, and his name was Jack Daniels. Why we followed Hogan instead of his contemporary and equal Byron Nelson, who didn't like to practice much (but didn't drink, either), is a damn good question, one we can talk about over a beer.

For half a century now, and increasingly each year, the heart of golf thumps on the broad, flat stage of the practice tee, where nothing counts but everything is crucial. Fear sucks the oxygen from the air, and the ticks and twitches of ritual fight off the butterflies. Professional golf had once been social, now it is withdrawn. Most people think it's the money, but it's not that simple.

Like an eighteenth-century battlefield, the range composes itself into skirmish lines. At the front, golfer/soldiers aim relentless fire at distant targets. They joke and banter with caddies and instructors about wine and women, and ask fellow competitors if they're playing at Milwaukee. But for some guys, on some days, the pressure wraps so tightly you could measure it in psi. Behind the warriors, support troops mingle uneasily, competing for a deal or a job or an interview while still watching the golfers with the preoccupied vigilance of mothers on the beach. The tension at the front rolls to the rear.

The fourth regiment in the range war gets its stress from the data streaming into its ears via cell phone. "We're down 6 percent versus the second quarter last year," the boss says. "Those bastards from Callaway and Titleist are up 5 percent. So we have a problem. *You* have a problem." Sincere men with insincere laughs, the equipment reps look over your shoulder when you talk with them, alert as bird dogs for a signal from a player to fetch him a club or to approach for a conference. Those come-hither gestures are pregnant with money, because amateurs play what the pros play. The golf equipment and apparel market is very volatile, and consumer loyalty has been crumbling for years.

The reps' weapons are vigilance, sunscreen, and golf bags crammed with drivers, woods, wedges, putters, and naked shafts. Often their collective wares sit like yard sale merchandise in a little roped-in paddock about twenty-five paces from the front. There, the navy and gray satchel of Fujikura Performance Shafts does silent battle with UST Proforce Gold Like No Other Shafts, and with Penley, and Aldila, and Rifle High Performance, and True-Temper WITH BI-MATRIX TECHNOLOGY. In clubs it's TaylorMade, Callaway, PING, Cleveland, Titleist, Hogan, Sonartec, Porsche Design, and the rest. If a player who usually plays a Porsche with a Penley decides to test-drive a Ping with a Proforce, four reps eye each other, and the player, and the flight of his golf balls against the sky. And calculate what will happen to their careers if this particular PGA Tour star joins or leaves the stable.

The media, the ants at this picnic, are of two distinct types, one frantic, the other watchful. Two- or three-person local TV crews rush and push and never seem to catch up. "Producer says we've got to get twenty-five seconds of the defending champ!" says the on-camera man or woman. "He was supposed to be here. Parnevik, you know, the guy with the funny hat? Brad, you know which one he is?" Brad the cameraman doesn't have a clue. He'll be shooting a traffic accident tomorrow, then a city council meeting. He's dressed for a hike, or to wash his Isuzu, or for beers at a place with sweaty floors. An hour ago, the on-camera man looked ready for his table at the Four Seasons, but now his makeup is melting from the pressure and the May Texas swelter.

Writers adopt a lower-key posture, similar to that of birdwatchers. They blend, they move slowly and quietly, and they ask if they may ask a few questions. Only camera- and soundmen rank lower sartorially. Equipment reps, instructors, and players dress for golf, with more blacks and navies this year than last, and more texture interest. Caddies wear baggy beige Bermuda shorts and running shoes. Wraparound sunglasses rest the eyes and hide anxiety for the first four groups. But the English majors who consider themselves the intellectuals of the practice tee have no time for the latest look, or not enough money. The hallmark of the writers' ensemble is the free golf shirt. An actual logo on one such garment, painted on, not stitched in: "Art

Sellinger Doritos Light Tortilla Chips Long Drive Pro-Am."

Unless it's the last few minutes before the final round of the U.S. Open or the PGA, the men and women from the national TV networks do not bother with the practice tee hubbub.

Who fears the media? Almost everyone on the tee—as much for the interruptions they represent as for what they might broadcast or write. But reporters are easy to block in most cases, either by being unavailable or by responding with no elaboration or with the worst clichés. Cold shoulders give writers the willies and reinforce their worst traits: insecurity, superiority, and a tendency to be judgmental, even vindictive.

Only one group moves with complete ease from the front of the range to the back fence. Agents—the generals in the range war—nod, wave, or speak to almost everyone. Smart guys, many of them lawyers or business school grads, their fashion sense and interpersonal skills are the best on the tee. For example, here's David Yates of Gaylord Sports Management, Scottsdale, Arizona, in a sky-blue pinpoint cotton long-sleeved dress shirt, charcoal-gray double-pleated slacks, hand-tooled leather belt with a metal tip, and handmade Italian loafers. He worked for fifteen years at International Management Group, the inventor of the sports agency and still by far the biggest player. He rose to VP and represented such as Nick Faldo, Bernhard Langer, and Mark Calcavecchia, so he's got the business part down. Once a prominent amateur golfer, he coached the sport at the United States Military Academy, Stanford, and the

University of Oklahoma. Tour player Andrew Magee graced his squad at OU. So Yates knows the golf part, too.

He shakes the hand of a player his old agency represents, and they chat for a moment. Then his eyes scan upward, to the top of a steep embankment twenty feet above the practice putting green, and he recognizes the head and shoulders of a former IMG colleague, Clarke Jones. Their eyes meet, or seem to. From Yates's point of view, Jones looks like a sniper in a coat and tie. But Jones pulls out a cell phone, not a rifle. And Yates is sure that Jones is calling back to IMG headquarters in Cleveland, to Alastair Johnston or to the founder, Mark McCormack, to report a seeming violation of the noncompete clause in Yates's exit agreement. "I'll talk to whoever I want to," Yates mutters at Jones, who is too far away to hear. Their eyes might have locked at this point, like those of duelists at high noon, had not each been wearing the inevitable, impenetrable sunglasses.

Friendships on the tee are really more like truces. Everyone affects a poker-faced coolness. Meanwhile, agents dread poaching from other agents, and indecision and lowball pricing from the club, shirt, shaft, and ball manufacturers with whom they are supposed to make endorsement deals, and the moods and whims of their clients. Equipment and apparel reps fear and mistrust each other, as do instructors, caddies, and writers. The players fear a thousand things, including fear itself, but mostly they're frightened of the future. And everyone's a little nervous about them, the sweating, incessantly practicing golfers at the front.

No one fears nothing. Except one man. Tiger.

Here he comes.

A few children skip before him in the late afternoon sun, as if to strew rose petals in the path of a new bride and groom. Like fighter jets escorting a bomber, four stern, uniformed men surround him. Caddie Steve Williams flies the point, walking fast, carrying a big black and white golf bag emblazoned BUICK. From nowhere—for it's 6:30 P.M. on a muggy Tuesday and the tournament doesn't begin until Thursday—a crowd appears. Down the hill Tiger strides, a lithe, slender athlete in baggy pants. Just got here from his home in Florida, in-the-know fans tell each other. Won the last time he played, of course, the Masters, and now he owns all four of the major trophies. No one's ever done that, except, I guess, Bobby Jones. How old is he now? Twenty-five? My God, a woman says, seeing him for the first time, he's *magnificent.* Is he, like . . . ? No, I think he dropped his girlfriend. Why, do you want to ask him out?

Past the practice putting green, through the ropes and onto the tee strides Eldrick T. Woods. With its proximity to bathrooms, the equipment reps, a chipping area, and the building housing the Byron Nelson Golf School, the right side of this tee is the social side. Tiger and Steve go left.

"No, no, *no, goddammit.* Speed it up," he says. Tiger is a mutterer. Another swing. "Faster!" Another. "Too fast. See, now it spins out. Match the swing and the hip." He's as profane as a Marine Corps DI, which may have something to do with two men: Earl, his father, and Butch

Harmon, his teacher, both of whom are Vietnam combat vets. Tiger cusses casually, making an unnatural suggestion to caddie Williams, or caustically tearing into himself on the practice tee with almost the same sincerity he showed in the heat of his most recent tournament. For example: "A flier," he'd snarled on the ninth fairway in the last round at the Masters. "Goddammit." A flier is an iron shot that goes too far because grass intervenes between club head and ball, reducing its spin. CBS's sophisticated audio equipment broadcast the monologue.

"Did he say what I think he said?" a ten-year-old student at a Catholic elementary school asked his father. "Yeah," the father replied, continuing to stare at the television. "And you can say that, too. The next time you're leading the Masters with nine to play."

For as Earl Woods told *Golf Digest*, "You can't have it both ways with Tiger. You can't have charismatic abilities to execute the marvelous shots and then chastise him when that same passion causes him to overload when he hits a bad shot." Besides, Earl said, swearing runs in the family. "My father could swear for thirty minutes and never repeat himself. He was that good."

No parent need fear that Tiger will corrupt America's youth. His intent and his effect is quite the opposite, and his overall presentation of success and wholesomeness is strong. As for the audible cussing, we tend to blame the boom mikes—for competitors this intense, and this successful, we'll cut some slack. After all, would Wheaties put a pretender on its box? Does Disney hire reprobates to endorse its TV networks? Unless he's caught in bed with a dead girl or a live boy, Woods has nothing to worry about in terms of image.

We love him. Corporate America pursues him with embarrassing ardor, so his endorsement income of $54 million in 2000 will probably increase as the old deals expire and new ones take their place. "I see him in two or three years going over $100 million annually in endorsements," says Bob Williams, president of Burns Sports and Celebrities. "There are some major categories he's not in: soft drinks, telecommunications, fast food. He's made no secret he loves the Golden Arches." And Taco Bell.

If Tiger follows in the footsteps of Michael Jordan and urges the world to eat more Big Macs, the deal will probably be brokered by his agent, International Management Group, of Cleveland, Ohio. The 1995 PGA champion, Steve Elkington, exaggerating a bit for effect, says that some day Tiger will be a kind of loss leader for his agency, "that IMG is going to be paying *him*." Perhaps the analogy is to the huge Mercedes Benz logo in front of its factory by I-95 in northern New Jersey, the most heavily traveled piece of road in the world. For being its glowing blue, forty-foot-high trademark, Tiger gets a special deal from IMG—a lower commission rate, a bit of stock—and he deserves it. Like Mercedes Benz, Tiger stands for excellence, and he acts as a magnet to draw other high earners to the agency. New and potential clients should ask why any of the best people at IMG would expend time on their behalf when they've already got a money machine in Tiger. But apparently they don't ask, or those smooth talkers from Cleveland explain away the conflict. Or make it seem like an advantage.

After five—at least—years with an agent (Earl let it slip in a TV interview that was never shown that Tiger was represented while still a student at Stanford, an egregious violation of NCAA rules), Woods enjoys a sunnier relationship with his representatives than do most golf pros. In fact, everyone close to him has the bouncy step of a Super Bowl winner. His instructor is like a brother to him; he calls Claude Harmon, Jr., Butchie, and Harmon calls him T or Teeg. Same deal with his caddie, Steve Williams—"Stevie"—a deep-voiced man's man from New Zealand who has the most pleasing ability to keep his mouth shut around the media, which his predecessor, Fluff Cowan, didn't. As for his parents, Tiger declared his independence by moving to the other side of the continent, to an extremely gated community near Orlando. Earl, seventy, beset with weight, heart, and ex-smoker problems, remains in the family home in Cypress, near Los Angeles. Now more the safety valve for Tiger than his spokesman, he coauthors books for the insatiable masses and handles some of the media overflow. He's also the president of his son's charity, the Tiger Woods Foundation, and the president of TWC Corporation. Tida lives in a new house in Tustin, a few miles from their old house. Earl describes the house Tiger bought for his mother as "large and showy . . . her dream home."

The happy team led to happy results. Into the spring of 2001, Tiger's golf game varied only between spectacular and superb. No worries there, either, only inspiration and possibility.

What about women? Are they a problem? Well, Tiger's

such a target that he's got to be careful about when and how he sneezes, much less who he dates. His is a scalp some women might brag about, perhaps ruining deals with G-rated companies like Disney, and his is a fortune many others would love to have access to. The locker room rumor is that Tiger felt obliged to pay his former squeeze Joanna Jagoda hush money when they split. But Woods knows some discreet women. When he visits Harmon, at his golf school in Las Vegas, he combines golf with girls and gambling. His new girlfriend is Swedish. He likes blondes.

Earl weighed in on the matrimonial issue in an interview with *TV Guide* in June. "I'd like to see him get married and have children," Woods Senior said. However, "I don't see Tiger marrying before thirty, if then. Let's face it—a wife can sometimes be a deterrent to a good game of golf. 'That's all you do is practice. Why don't you stay home here and have some quality time with me.' 'Honey, I'm a professional golfer.' 'Well, I'm your wife.' "

Tiger smiled indulgently at this, handling it perfectly, because the child is becoming father to the man. "That's just my dad," he said. "I'll know when it's time to settle down."

The media can be as bad as the nagging wife Earl pictures, and some segments of it are particularly curious about things he or anyone would rather keep private. Tiger defends with scheduled news conferences, by paying more attention to TV than to print, by ignoring questions posed incorrectly or at the wrong time, and by being generally unavailable. A writer who wanted to get a few minutes in April was told by IMG gatekeeper Bev Norwood that the list of those wanting a chat was so impossibly long that no names could be added to it. In August, the list had become impossibly short; in fact, it had been eliminated. And no, he won't ask Tiger to give you five minutes. "The only way to talk to him," said Norwood, a slight man of late middle years who has made his diffidence a strength, "is to hang around and ask your questions."

But "hang around and ask your questions" usually means joining a demeaning scrum around the superstar when he ventures for a moment into the open field. Thoughtful questions and reasoned replies are difficult, and woe unto the reporter whose question is not of general interest. You'd better not ask about the role of Buddhism in Tiger's life, for example, when everyone else wants to hear about the eagle putt on the ninth hole. If you're a part of this cluster with a notebook or a tape recorder or a camera, you feel like a beggar chasing a rickshaw. (Worse, you might recall that Princess Diana spent her last moments alive fleeing such as yourself.) Tiger in this situation can be charming or disdainful, depending upon how he played. But he always seems a bit preoccupied, and a little bit nervous.

He'd prefer to get the media chore over with, if he can, with a Q and A near the scorer's trailer. He walks to a certain point, and writers and photographers surround him like iron filings around a magnet. Doug Ferguson, the AP writer whom Tiger likes and respects, is nominally in charge: At least he asks the most questions. Sometimes these interviews devolve into the lowest form of conversation, the walk-and-talk. In May, at the Nelson, we found out how low the walkabout can go. Media clotted around Tiger the instant he breached the yellow rope by the eighteenth green after his practice round, and he walked as fast as he could to the safety of the locker room, uphill and a hundred yards away. He heard the usual questions—"How was the course today? How do you think you'll do this week?"—but a reporter for an off-brand TV network didn't want to go there. "What about the Texas women, Tiger? How do you think they compare to the girls in California or Florida?" Woods ignored the reporter, who ran alongside, rephrased the question, and asked again. And again. "That's it, buddy, I'm done," he finally said to the reporter. Then Tiger added in a whisper we could all hear, "Fucking idiot." And we agreed.

Things are always warmer for Tiger on the Golf Channel, with which he enjoys a special relationship. He lives nearby in Orlando and has often driven uninvited to the studio in his white Porsche, to sit in a room to watch tapes of old golf tournaments and TV exhibition matches. He's also been a frequent guest, of course. "I made a few mistakes," Tiger told host Peter Kessler in an interview in March of '97. "You're allowed to at your age," Kessler said. "You're allowed to at twice your age." Tiger pursed his lips. "Yeah, I know," he said. "Unfortunately the public and the media don't seem to look at it that way."

The turning point in his press relations occurred in 1997 when he met a *Gentlemen's Quarterly* writer named Charles P. Pierce. Pierce hung with Tiger for a couple of days, watched him play in and win the first event on the

Tour in '97, the Mercedes Championship. The story, entitled "The Man. *Amen*," portrayed Woods as a triple contradiction, an all-too-human twenty-one-year-old golf savior. Pierce filled the piece with the shout-and-response phrasings of a black Baptist church on Sunday morning and repeated again and again the words "gospel" and "blasphemy" and "faith." He communicated the all-too-human part by repeating verbatim some sexual jokes with racial overtones Tiger told to a limo driver and to a couple of young, pretty photographer's assistants.

Tiger and Company read what he said and that was the end of his public candor. He clammed up, or wised up, and developed an impressively empty kind of media speech that still fills up notebooks and tape. He prefaces a lot of his sentences with the word "obviously," a clear signal that the words to come will contain no surprises. "Obviously, I'd like to win. Obviously, I'm playing well." He understands the power of editing, so he'll do a bit of live TV after his round but blow off Ed Bradley and *60 Minutes*. For another example, *Newsweek* wanted to talk a couple of weeks before the U.S. Open. For our June 18 cover, their people told his people. No can do, Eldrick said. *Newsweek* went ahead anyway, using a four-year-old photo of that extraordinary face on the cover below an appropriate headline: TIGER RULES.

Or does he? Since the First Amendment to the Constitution forbids Congress and IMG from making any laws abridging the freedom of the press, Tiger must endure things such as what appeared in Walter Scott's Personality Parade, *Parade* magazine, August 27, 2001:

Q: You implied that Tiger Woods and his longtime girlfriend are no longer together. What is his romantic status?

A: Confusing. Woods, 25, broke up with Joanna Jagoda, 23, earlier this year. He later was seen in Vegas, giving golf tips to Gabrielle Reece, 31, the volleyball star and model. When the tabloids hinted at a romance, Reece denied it, saying she had reconciled with her husband. . . .

He's in *Parade,* he's in *People.* He's in the tabloids at the supermarket checkout, competing for attention against the AMAZING BUT TRUE story of the three-breasted woman and her three-armed husband, proud parents of a three-legged baby. In one of these, the August 28 *Star* (the number-one Celebrity News Magazine, according to itself), next to a head shot of Tiger and a photo of a spade royal flush, the tabloid shouted this headline: TIGER WOODS GAMBLING AWAY HIS MILLIONS! "Golf phenomenon Tiger Woods has lost so many millions of dollars gambling in Las Vegas that his beloved father fears that the young golfing great may be turning into a compulsive gambler," wrote Jill Ishkanian. "He hits the gaming tables whenever he's on a jaunt with his superstar pals, like former basketball superstars Michael Jordan and Charles Barkley." Ishkanian quoted a "sports insider" who said, "I think they're all gambling junkies. Gambling is their off-court thrill, and they've introduced Tiger to it. And he's taken to it like he took to golf."

But the prying press may as well be a million miles away

as Tiger continues to practice. Pink and purple paint the sky in fuzzy streaks, and the crowd slowly thins. Beneath his shirt, the gold Buddha on a chain around his neck sways and jumps with every swing. Sweat soaks his made-in-Peru, double-mercerized, two-ply cotton Nike shirt from his thickly muscled shoulders to his tailbone, and the clinging fabric convinces you that his is not the body of an athlete but of a dancer. Who else but a guy in the ABT or the Bolshoi could possess such a combination of flexibility and strength? He's Nureyev with a metal stick and a white plastic ball, perfectly balanced and full of grace while executing a split-second flex of fifty muscles.

Tiger's the last one on the range, which is not to say that he practiced longer than the other guys. He hits the driver last. If a spectator positions himself just so, he can watch Tiger's Nike golf balls fly into the glowing disc of the rising moon. And if the spectator doesn't watch himself, he might imagine ET on a flying bicycle, or recall Yeats's words about flight, "a lonely impulse of delight."

Finally Tiger gets inside his security formation for the walk up to the hotel, which is on the grounds here at the Four Seasons in Irving, Texas. In his $1,500 top-floor, two-bedroom suite, he picks up the phone and talks to room service. A few minutes later, his food arrives—a peanut butter and banana sandwich on white, and a glass of milk. A happy meal after a long day.

PLAYERS, INSTRUCTORS, CADDIES, reps, agents, media, fans, and behind them, junior golfers and their parents—if golf is a layer cake, then Tiger's the little tuxedoed figure on top. Each level feels the weight of his tread.

To some his footsteps sound like there's a fat man jumping rope on the roof. Others claim not to hear a thing. "Chasing Tiger?" asks Andrew Magee. "I'm chasing Gary McCord." McCord plays the Senior Tour and plays the court jester on the CBS broadcasts of golf tournaments. Magee's humor is as witty and glib as McCord's and he's just as articulate and insightful. But his slightly nasal voice doesn't modulate as well: He'd have to work on that. On the other hand, he's got a hell of a lot more hair. He's about to turn forty and for the first time in his life, he's feeling old. This wouldn't be the last time in 2001 that Magee talked about career options. Because for the first time in his life, he's failing at something.

"My business isn't very good," Magee says, his way of saying that he hasn't been playing well. It's April 22 and he's on the practice green at the Shell Houston Open. For two hours with one club and three golf balls. April 22 and he's won only $40,533. This is a man who's been within shouting distance of a million dollars a year in prize money the previous three years. But in 2001 he's missed the cut in five of the nine tournaments he's entered. He's paid Uncle Sam about a third of the forty in taxes, and it costs three to four thousand a week to travel and live on the Tour. Magee's operating in the red and everyone knows it.

Since 1985, his first full year on the Tour, he hasn't endured a bad slump. With failure a mere abstraction, he quite naturally built a financial life based on a high income.

He's got a daughter in college, mortgages on two houses, a wife who likes Pashmina and stargazer lilies, two other kids, and a couple of dogs. Endorsement income keeps him afloat, but Coors Light won't continue paying him at the same level to wear its logo on his shirt if he never plays well enough to get on TV on Saturday and Sunday. The easy money of the Senior Tour is still ten years away. His career truly is at a crossroads.

"So I guess you're looking at some of the younger guys," Magee says, while continuing to experiment with a midlength putter, one end of which he buries in his belly button as he strokes Spalding golf balls at a hole. "Charles Howell? Perfect."

While Magee claims not to feel affected by Tiger in the slightest, Charles Howell III can't remember the time when he didn't have Tiger on his mind, at least a little bit. "I want to beat him," he says. "I want to be the best in the world." He makes waves by uttering these thoughts, because hardly anyone else dares to. Can he back it up? When the PGA Tour comes to a town near you, go out and watch Howell and see what you think. Even if you conclude he doesn't have the putter to topple Tiger, there's entertainment in seeing someone as young (twenty-two) and thin as a Gap model drive the ball longer and straighter than Woods. Longer and straighter than anyone. He sets the ball on an extra-long peg about four inches in the air, digs in his spikes like he's about to attempt a standing broad jump, and then whips the titanium into the ball as if it's just said something about his mama. Even before he finishes his swing his Callaway Red is already one hundred yards away and it's departing so quickly it looks as small as a Tic Tac. But somehow, he never, ever loses his balance.

He's an aw-shucks young man despite his patrician-sounding name, from the home of golf (or one of them) in the United States, Augusta, Georgia. Despite the aw-shucks, he earned straight A's at Westminster Prep, where the academics are really tough, and a 3.76 at Oklahoma State, where they're not. If Woods hadn't sucked all the media attention from golf in the last few years, you'd have heard of him. But golf fans in Portland, Oregon, cannot forget the very skinny kid and the golf game he brought to Waverly Country Club for what would be the third of Tiger's three consecutive U.S. Juniors. Howell, fourteen, appeared younger than that, almost too young to be so far from home, competing in this company. He wore glasses then, and the frames seemed too big for the thin kid beneath them: He looked like Mr. Peepers. Woods, on the other hand, except for the layers of muscle he's added recently to arms and shoulders, looked a lot like he does now. When Tiger held up the trophy, he was a few months from his eighteenth birthday and just a few weeks from entering Stanford.

Perhaps, by the time we got to Howell, we thought we'd heard his story before. And in a way, we had. Like Woods, Howell focused on golf almost from the cradle, enjoyed sensational junior and college careers, won the NCAA, then quit school early to turn pro. Tiger lasted two years at Stanford when he bid farewell to men's golf coach Wally Goodwin. Charles gave Coach Mike Holder three years at Oklahoma State, but his leaving was less amicable. Howell turned pro without consulting his coach, and Holder felt left in the lurch. Both Tiger and Charles are skinny but strong, chose their parents well, practice as many hours as they sleep, train with weights, and employ the best instructors to shape their swings. Nike paid Tiger $10 million a year before he hit his first ball as a professional; Callaway ponied up about $2 million annually for Charles. Both men compete with an intensity that's so pure and bright it's almost hard to look at.

But they are not cut from the same cloth. Tiger mistrusts the media and can give fans little time; Howell, perhaps naively, signs every autograph and responds thoughtfully and at length to a reporter's questions. He says he's flattered that anyone would ask what he thinks. After hearing Howell agree enthusiastically to an interview request, Doug Ferguson of the AP sighs, "Why can't they all be like that?" And while Tiger plays the field, Charles got married this summer on the beach at Maui to a green-eyed beauty from Kingfisher, Oklahoma, Heather Myers.

Woods and Howell met head to head once, in the United States Amateur at Pumpkin Ridge in Oregon in 1996. Tiger was twenty, Charles, sixteen. The older boy won three-and-one, and went on to win the tournament. They didn't become friends. Both wanted the same thing then and now, to be the best. A Pennsylvania Dutch expression applies: "If they weren't so much alike they'd like each other."

Howell will not be quoted saying anything negative about Tiger. He's too polite and his background is too conservative and Christian to permit any trash talk. But a request that started as a joke then became another item on his to-do list, and thus a minor obsession: "Why don't you put me on the cover of your book? I'd be more accessible, and I'd give you much better quotes. If I win a tournament, you've got to put me on the cover."

As the year went on and his challenge gained more and more credibility, the national media discovered Howell. *ESPN Magazine*, *Sports Illustrated*, and the Golf Channel all did features on the Thin Man from Augusta. With his yes sirs and no sirs and genial disposition, he emerged as a very likable young man but with a monkish single-mindedness that was hard to fathom. He'd had no real friends in high school, he admitted. No girlfriend. And not a single date—no wait, he did borrow the car and Dad's aftershave once, when he went to the senior prom with a lovely girl, Fran Gardner. But someone else set the whole thing up—he couldn't finish high school without having at least *one* date, could he?—and his mother practically had to force him out the door. But he had a pretty good time and he came home with a crown on his head. In an ironic gesture, his classmates made the friendly but friendless, famous but famously antisocial golfer prom king. He put the crown on top of one of the scores of giant golf trophies in his bedroom.

"Why don't you date?" his mother, Deborah, asked him a hundred times. "Girls cause bogies, Mom," Charles would say. Deborah rolled her eyes at her son's tunnel vision. Where did he get that line? Must have been adapted from what Burgess Meredith—as Mick the trainer—had said in *Rocky*: "Women weaken legs." Just like his father, she thought, both the intensity of focus and the dry, sly humor. She herself had been among the most popular kids at her high school in Augusta, Richmond Academy, but her son made no room for a social life. The other kids wore blue jeans, the uniform and symbol of the casual life. Charles didn't own a single pair. He got his first denim pants during his second year at Oklahoma State, a gift from a roommate. He still has them.

"I started playing golf when I was seven, and it wasn't just for the heck of it," Charles says. "After the first day I played, I came home and said I wanted lessons."

And at that crucial moment of his young life, his father listened.

JUNIOR GOLFERS COMPARE themselves to one another, or their parents do, as relentlessly as beauty pageant competitors. It's not as cut and dried as money won or world rankings, of course, but it's close. *Golfweek*, the junior's Bible, rates the top one hundred U.S. golfers age eighteen and under. The *Golfweek* Hot One Hundred is the scorecard in a game with almost absurdly high stakes. It's not that the kids are competing for college scholarships—they are, but that's nothing new and it's hardly unique to golf. And it's not that most of the kids think they're on their way to playing with Tiger in the last group at the Masters. That's not new, either. Athletic fantasy has been around since the first newspaper sports page: a desire to hit a baseball like Rogers Hornsby animated my father's life in

Chicago in 1930, and a lot of us in Ohio in 1970 made firm plans to be very much like Jack Nicklaus. Or Tom Weiskopf, minimum.

Where the equation has really changed is not in how much the kids gamble—hell, they've got time, and dedication to a game as rewarding as golf is almost always a good thing—it's in how much the parents risk. Junior golf has gone big time, and you can thank or blame the Woods family for turning a trend into an obsession. Tiger won the lottery—and keeps winning it—in part by having started his competitive career at age three and taking lessons beginning at age four. And damn the expense, wrote Earl in *Playing Through*: "Tida and I made a personal commitment to each other that we would devote all of our energies and finances to assure that he had the best we could give him. Total commitment! Well, something had to give, and it was our relationship. The priority became Tiger, and not each other."

Why a couple would sacrifice the union that made the kid possible in the first place is a complicated issue. Part of it must be a laudable selflessness and love. Perhaps deep down Earl resembled the mother of one of the twentieth century's greatest poets, Edna St. Vincent Millay. "It's striking how many writers of both sexes have been the offspring of mothers like Cora Millay," wrote Judith Thurman in *The New Yorker* (September 3, 2001). "Exceptional women disappointed in marriage and thwarted in ambition and desire who give all and ask for nothing except that the special child live gloriously enough for two."

Whatever the motivation, parents can express their deep

commitment easily enough. Junior golf has its own tour, the American Junior Golf Association, and all the hotel, gasoline, car repair, food, and airline expenses implied by the word "tour." Tiger played AJGA and to some extent popularized it. The expense seems staggering. The touring junior needs new clubs every now and then at about six hundred dollars per set, an instructor at about a hundred dollars an hour, probably a country club membership at God-knows-how-much, and new clothes—and forget Old Navy, these kids wear Polo. One or both parents attend most of the tournaments, most of the time, often sacrificing a couple of days' pay or vacation days. Some of the parents, following Earl's blueprint, employ a mental coach for their embryo pro. And trainers. And, so help me, nutritionists. Total commitment!

Recently Charles Howell calculated what his parents had spent to help make him the world's number-one-ranked junior, and then the top or almost the top-ranked amateur, an exercise that illustrated both Howell's precision and the upper-end cost for a young player's climb to the top. Recall that Charles didn't develop a desire to be the best in the world, he started with it. And remember, too, that his father understood his son's ambition and decided not to impede his son's progress with half measures. Like any good physician, Dr. Howell knew how to find the best specialists, so Charles's first lessons were with the highly recommended George Kellner Hoffer at the Atlanta Golf Center, a two-and-a-half-hour drive from Augusta. At age ten, his son's dedication and talent confirmed, Dr. Howell raised the stakes, and switched Charles from a very good instructor to possibly the best one, David Leadbetter. Getting Charles to Leadbetter's lesson tee in Orlando with some regularity was not cheap.

Charles figured the average annual expenses for travel, equipment, lessons, clothes, entry fees, and membership at Augusta Country Club, and multiplied by twelve years. He adjusted for inflation, interest rate, opportunity cost, and the time value of money (he took macroeconomics at OSU and got an A). The final number: about eight hundred thousand dollars.

Most parents will spend far less, of course, if only because most people make a lot less than a top pediatric surgeon. Chasing Tiger can annihilate the family budget—and the family. Sometimes the highest cost is the emotional one.

"I saw a mother kick her kid right in the rear end," recalls Mike Cassell, who, with his father, founded one of the big events, the Hudson Junior Invitational in Ohio. Phil Mickelson, Magee, Billy Andrade, and a handful of other current touring pros played in Hudson. "I also saw a father yank on his son's arm so hard after a three-putt that I thought he might pull it out of its socket. But with the really good players, you didn't even notice that their parents were there."

As to that last point, the Howells had a different experience with at least two high-profile juniors and their high-pressure fathers. "There's this one—you know who he is, but I'm not gonna say his name—who liked to go on the practice tee and make comments to the kids who might beat his kid," recalls Dr. Howell. "He'd say 'Hey, I noticed that new move you've got at the top of your backswing—sure looks good,' or, 'When did you change your grip? I liked the way you had it before.' "

Deborah Howell shudders to remember another father of another very high-profile junior golfer who "just berated his son. In a *loud* voice. He'd jab his index finger into his boy's chest, and say something like, 'You're playing like an idiot! When are you gonna straighten up?' Awful. He got kicked out of more than one tournament."

Ron Balicki, who covers juniors and colleges for *Golfweek*, has seen all this and more. "A parent sent an e-mail to one of the reps I know, asking for free equipment. Said his kid was gonna be really good. The kid's *three.*" Balicki believes that Tiger has affected the parents more than their children. "They see what might happen if you start a kid before he's in kindergarten," he says, "but they don't see reality. They don't understand that Tiger was a special case, the best junior golfer ever. *Ever.*

"From taking golf so seriously at such a young age, they're taking the fun out of it. Burnout's just inevitable. You see it all the time. Those Wongluekiet kids who've been so good? At the U.S. Junior, one of them lost in the first round, and the other didn't even qualify for match play. You wouldn't believe how intense the kids are at these tournaments. And how intense their parents are."

Intensity is one thing, abuse is another. But because of the game itself—its honor system, its do-unto-others behavior code—golf will always compare well to other sports. Take baseball, for example. Scolding and profane parents with their egos on the line have been ruining youth leagues for years. Baseball tradition emboldens adults to swear at the umpire and to try to rattle the eleven-year-olds on the other team, life lessons of dubious value. Not coincidentally, it costs only fifty bucks or so to get a kid into a Little League uniform for an entire season—versus the $150 per tournament charged by the AJGA. Basketball parents can be just as bad as baseball, but seldom are, thank goodness. Many hockey and soccer moms and dads should be sedated before being allowed to watch. Overbearing tennis parents trying to get their little miss or mister on the pro tour are legend.

When junior golf parents snap from the pressure, they may be reacting to the money they've just spent at the Holiday Inn or to the frustratingly high standard set by Tiger, but they are not following the example of Earl and Tida. Their behavior as spectators was flawless: Perhaps the fact that their son was always winning relaxed them. Mrs. Woods usually seemed to be the happiest person in any gallery. A light and lively woman, she wore big conical Thai-style sun hats and talked while she walked, and hung on the arm of whoever she was speaking with. She often kept score for Tiger and the other kids in his group and cheered for each one. Earl watched the action more keenly from behind wraparound shades. Between the sunglasses, his naturally down-turned mouth, and a vaguely military bearing, Earl owned an intimidating presence. But his girth made him look silly in shorts and the shortness of breath from his cigarette habit caused him to walk very slowly and made him less forbidding. He was patient and pleasant with strangers who asked him how to raise their own Tiger. "First," Earl would always say, "put a golf club in his crib."

GOLF GAVE TIGER WOODS the boy purpose, identity, and a stage. It filled his heart with the wonderful feeling that he was doing exactly what he was born to do, and that his success pleased the two people he most wanted to please. But Tiger the man wants to dismantle golf and start over.

He revealed his deep discontent in December 1996, a few days before his twenty-first birthday, in an interview with Peter Kessler on the Golf Channel. We were still early in Tigermania back then, and Kessler asked Tiger to describe his goals. "To be the best golfer that I can be—that's a given," said Woods, who wore a gray wide-wale corduroy cap, with the brim in the back, and a large white Nike logo sewn in the nominal front and facing the camera. "As I've grown up and matured and gotten more of a perspective on life, one of my main goals is to make golf look like America." The second half of his response was surprising both for its content and for sounding strangely canned, like Clinton saying "grow the economy" or Bush vowing "to leave no child behind."

Explain, Kessler said.

"How many kids do you see at the ballpark or at the playground playing hoop who are of all different races?" replied Tiger. "They gather everywhere and they just do it. I want golf to be the same way. It's such a great game, why limit it to just a few, when it can be enjoyed by all?"

The question sounded skillfully rhetorical and idealistic—

why *can't* we provide a prescription drug benefit for the elderly?—but required a fight through several layers of cynicism. The first grain of salt came from the comparison of two playground sports—requiring little more than a ball and a hoop, or a ball and a bat—with golf. Baseball is a kid's game that adults sometimes play but golf is an adult game that some kids can learn. The average age of a golf beginner in the United States is thirty-something, possibly because the tuition is exponentially higher than anything on the playground. The equipment is elaborate, the rules are arcane, and etiquette and comportment are crucial. Basketball requires a patch of blacktop and a goal; to build even the most no-frills golf course costs $2 million. New golfers need to have some money, in other words, a lot of time, and even more patience.

The logo on his hat delivered another argument against the words coming out of his mouth. And that phrase he used—"Just do it." After seeing the swoosh and hearing Tiger say the catch phrase from their infinitely repeated ad campaign, you had to wonder what was in it for Nike. Since he wears their symbol virtually all the time, and since they pay him $10 million a year, it's reasonable to assume he's always selling, that everything Tiger says is a commercial message. "I want basically to give kids in the inner city—in any city really—the chance to play a beautiful game," Tiger concluded. It sounded like the New Products for New Markets strategy they teach in the first college marketing class. Was Tiger/Nike cloaking a business purpose in altruism? They teach that gambit in the second class: OmniBank will donate a portion of your December charges to the World Wildlife Fund. Clip the labels off your soup cans and Campbell's will give money to your school. Buy Nike and help the angry and the alienated in the concrete jungle.

A cynic might also wonder why making golf look like America—less white, presumably, and more black and brown—was a worthy goal. Should racial quotas be extended to all sports, from the nine on the field for the Yankees to the five on the floor for the Lakers? Of course not: Obviously Tiger's wish concerned opportunity, not the colors of the best players. Yet here was a man with caramel-colored skin, sitting on top of golf and a mountain of money. For him, at least, the system appeared to be working.

Was he pushing someone else's agenda? You don't picture golf's Mozart having suffered at the hands of racist America. Yet he says, "I was always treated as an outsider." Like a lonely raisin in a rice pudding, the Woods family stood out in their otherwise all-white neighborhood in suburban Los Angeles. He got into a fight the first day of kindergarten. "I've been denied a lot of things just because of the color of my skin—whether school, socially, or in golf. That's just the way it was." A driving range pro kicked him off the premises in 1994, he said, because the owner of a nearby house had complained that "this little nigger" was hitting balls over a fence and onto his roof. Tiger could have hit balls through the man's window and into his soup if he wanted to, but he was not the guilty party.

Despite Nike, and new markets, and the wealth and success he had already achieved, Tiger's dissatisfaction with the face of golf was genuine. He'd absorbed all the outrages endured by his father, and he had some of his own, and then he met Charlie Sifford. Like his father, Sifford loved a smoke and jazz and a drink. "I treat Charlie like he's my grandfather," Tiger said. "I love him dearly."

Although his friends and family say he's got a lovable side, on most days Sifford, almost eighty, is about the grouchiest man alive. Don't try to interview him. Four out of five times—an actual count, not a figurative one—he not only will not answer your questions, he will make you feel one inch high for asking them. He's got an excuse for his gruffness, however. As a black man trying to make a living on the postwar golf tour, he suffered through an appalling amount of racially motivated insult and disrespect. As Tiger would discover, Grandpa Charlie was the reluctant and angry star of the PGA of America's most shameful chapter.

The newspapers back in the day referred to him as "Cigar-chomping Charlie Sifford, the four-time National Negro Open Champion." He had a funny punch of a swing but he controlled the ball like it was a yo-yo on a string. He had the game, in other words, to compete and win at the highest level. But blacks were not welcome in every PGA tournament (the PGA Tour, a spinoff from the PGA, did not begin until 1968). According to Article III, Section 1, of the Constitution and By-Laws of the Professional Golfers' Association of America: "Professional golfers of the Caucasian race, over the age of 18, residing in North or South America, who can qualify under the terms and conditions hereinafter specified, shall be eligible for membership." The infamous whites-only clause stood until Sifford, the NAACP, and California attorney general Stanley Mosk contrived to get it off the books in 1961. But Charlie's fight had only just begun.

For the first time in his career—Charlie was already thirty-eight—the Bing Crosby Pro-Am and Palm Springs tournaments invited him to compete in '61, thanks in part to the intercession of Jackie Robinson, Joe Louis, and his old friend and patron, the black Frank Sinatra, Billy Eckstine. But after the events in Phoenix and Tucson, the tour followed its usual path east to Baton Rouge, New Orleans, Puerto Rico, Pensacola, St. Petersburg, Palm Beach, and Wilmington, North Carolina. Sifford applied to enter all these tournaments. None accepted him.

Then came the Masters, and then the Greater Greensboro Open, and Charlie felt he had the same chance to play in those as to sprout wings and fly. But the head of the Greensboro NAACP pulled some strings and got Sifford in. He would be the first black man to play in a PGA tournament in the South. It was a disaster.

He drove from his home in Los Angeles to North Carolina, lonely and full of dread. Good hotels accepting people of color were hard to find in Greensboro, or didn't exist, so he took a room in a dormitory at an all-black college, North Carolina A&T. School was still in session and the dorm was noisy as hell, but Charlie shot 68 in the first round and led the tournament. That night he accepted an offer from a sympathetic black family, the Lavetts, and happily left NC A&T. Things were looking up. But somehow, from out of the darkness, they found him. The Lavetts' phone rang. "It's for you, Charlie." "You'd better not bring your black ass out to no golf course tomorrow if you know what's good for you, nigger," a hateful voice said. "You'd just better watch out, nigger."

Sifford froze: Except for a few stares, the first day of the Greater Greensboro Open had gone smoothly. "Suddenly, things had changed," he wrote in his vivid and heartfelt autobiography, *Just Let Me Play.* "It wasn't a golf tournament I was in, it was a war zone . . . I couldn't shake the fear. I knew how easily black people could disappear in the South." A wolf pack of young white men stalked him the next day, shouting, taunting—"go back to the cotton fields"—until security finally led them away by the fourteenth green. Under the circumstances, Sifford's fourth-place finish was remarkable. Mike Souchak won. Charlie drove to Texas, with his check for thirteen hundred dollars from Greensboro.

Things got worse. Houston had the next event on the suddenly integrated tour. But in the clubhouse at Memorial Park Golf Course, a man representing the sponsors of the Houston Classic informed him he would not be playing, and a PGA official could only say, "Sorry, Charlie." Furious, he drove the Houston streets aimlessly for an hour. At the Texas Open at Oak Hill in San Antonio the next week, Sifford couldn't even get past the guard at the gate. He put his Cadillac in reverse and headed back to California.

Imagine Tiger sitting with Charlie as he told these and other stories through his cigar smoke. About frequently having to eat his lunch on a bench in front of his locker, smelling sweaty shoes and damp towels, because some clubs would not allow him in their restaurants. About the tournaments that tacked on an extra word at the end of their names, just to keep the only black pro out. The Texas Open, for example, became the nonsensical and contradictory Texas Open Invitational to give its exclusion of Sifford a whiff of legality.

Four months after the face of America interview, Woods electrified the sports world by winning the Masters by twelve shots, the widest victory margin in the history of golf's four majors. It was as if the Cleveland Indians had won the seventh game of the World Series 30–0.

He was the first person of color to win the tournament. He mentioned Sifford's name in his victory remarks, and two of Charlie's predecessors, Teddy Rhodes and Bill Spiller, nearly forgotten men who were to golf what Satchel Paige and Cool Papa Bell had been to baseball. Which is to say, great players few of us got to see.

Seven months after that, on a cold, sunny November day in Central Park, a band of dignitaries—including former president George Bush—announced a new program to provide "affordable golf access for everyone, especially kids, who otherwise might not have an opportunity to play." The initiative of five of golf's biggest administrators—the same five who'd built the World Golf Hall of Fame—would be called the First Tee. It was so close to what the new king had been talking about that many people assumed it was his idea and his organization.

It wasn't. "He's given clinics and exhibitions at some

of our openings, but the First Tee didn't really have anything to do with Tiger or Earl," says First Tee spokesperson Amy Caruso. "Its founders are the PGA Tour, the USGA, the LPGA, the PGA of America, and Augusta National.

"But sure, Tiger's had a tremendous impact on us and on the game of golf. Look at TV viewership when he plays. He's brought golf to the masses. He's made kids and minorities believe, 'Hey, I can do it too.' "

Late in 2001, the First Tee was operating seventy-two kid-friendly facilities and had fifty-nine more in development. In addition to learning some golf, First Tee kids take complementary courses in "life skills," in which instructors draw parallels between the decision-making in golf and making choices in school and on the street.

It's a bold social experiment with an impressive group of backers. Very rich backers: the PGA of America milks a cash cow called the Ryder Cup; Augusta National swims in money from the billboard it rents to CBS every spring; and the Tour and the USGA have many millions of discretionary dollars after expenses. And none of them pay taxes! They've got to give it away.

Will it work? If it doesn't, there is an alternative way to get poor kids into golf, the path Charlie Sifford walked as a stocky twelve-year-old in Charlotte. He learned where to stand, how to act, when to talk, how to read a putt—all of the thousands of nuances in this lifestyle game played by presidents, prime ministers, and plumbers—and he didn't have to pay a dime. In fact, they paid him. Self-sufficiency, pride—he learned all the Boy

Scout virtues, plus valuable lessons in economics and what happens to a fool and his money. He learned the culture of golf, in other words, not just the game. It was a great system.

Charlie was a caddie.

THE FIRST TEE AUGUSTA opened dramatically on Tuesday of Masters Week 2001. Searchlights and a big floodlit tent amplified the feeling of portent, and the warm, gently scented night air made you feel like falling in love. Hundreds of recently bathed and well-dressed people milled around, smiling and waving at friends and looking to see who else they knew. There's Arnie, someone said. Arnold Palmer, forever the King in Augusta, would be saying a few words. His design firm had laid out the six-hole course and its practice range, no charge. One rumor floated in the air like the magnolia's perfume, namely, that Tiger would be there.

The speakers stood in front of the Doric-columned portico at the front of the bright white clubhouse. They said what they say on such occasions, that this was a laudable project, that it represented a tremendous amount of effort and foresight by the people who'd donated their time and money. And can we have a big hand for the chairman of the Fore!Augusta Foundation board of directors, Mr. Paul S. Simon. The second-to-last speaker recognized the outstanding golf pros in the audience, such as Augusta's own Franklin Langham. But no one from the podium recognized Charles Howell, who stood with his father and the pro from the Augusta municipal golf course, Guy Reid. Howell was having a miserable week. A hometown boy, as good as he was, and he hadn't been asked to play in the Masters. "Saw you on TV on Sunday, Cholls," his friends would say, gripping his elbow or his hand. "Finished sixth? What you win, hundred and three thousand? Sure wish you were playing this week." Howell would say thanks, thanks a lot. "My invitation must have gotten lost in the mail," he told everyone who asked, but he was getting sick of his own joke.

Speeches over, the happy crowd lined up for barbecue, potato salad, cole slaw, beans, bread, cobbler, and tea. Isn't this brisket good? we asked each other. Didn't they do a great job on this place? You think Tiger's gonna show up? You think he's gonna win? You meet Mayor Bob Young and his lovely wife Gwen, and say hey to former mayor Larry Sconyers, who catered this delicious meal. Still under the misapprehension that Tiger owned the First Tee, as the evening went on some people became miffed that the host did not seem to be showing up for his own party. Others counted the mere two handfuls of black people in attendance and concluded that this was a bad sign for a project designed to benefit inner-city youth.

In the silence that fell as people attacked the cobbler, there was time to wonder about Tiger and his putative brothers and sisters in their lousy houses downtown. Not so much what they thought of him—there are so many downtowns, and each downtown speaks with many voices. A better question would be what he thinks of them. He grew up in a white neighborhood, went to white schools, dated white girls, and became famous in a white sport. He is not a black man. Refer to him that way only if you want to make him furious.

"The media in general have always said that I was black," Tiger said in 1996. "I couldn't stand that. If you said I was purely black, then you're insulting my mom. And that is wrong. I will not accept it, I will not put up with it. Because I love my mom."

Where's Tiger? a latecomer asks. Did he ever show?

No, you answer. But he was here.

2

THE TUNA MINT

There is all the difference in the world between having something to say and having to say something.

—John Dewey

The radio studio at the corner of Broad Street and James Brown Boulevard in downtown Augusta sports a retro look, like the all-night coffee shop in *The Night Hawks.* But unlike the mute and preoccupied figures in George Bellows's famous painting, the man who stalks around the control panel and the microphones at Soul 94.7 announces his presence with a phosphorescent grace. The Boss. Window-shopping tourists often stop in their tracks and say, "Isn't that?" James Brown waves at them and smiles, and you almost want to throw a protective arm in front of your eyes at the flash of white teeth.

Fifty-one weeks a year Brown is the most famous black man—no, the most famous man—in Augusta, Georgia.

But now Eldrick Woods comes to town and people want to know what Brother James thinks of this kid.

It's cool and dim in the lobby of the radio station on the hot Tuesday afternoon of Masters Week, a day after the grand opening of First Tee Augusta, and two days before the first round of the tournament. A porcine security man with shaggy blond hair and a holstered sidearm moves his heavy lids up and down as you enter, checking you out. Then he stands back, just out of reach of a column of sunlight shining through the front door. There's been some trouble lately. Someone—allegedly a disgruntled former employee—pitched a firebomb onto the roof of James Brown Enterprises, a red brick building over on Augusta West Parkway. The bomb burned a bathtub-sized hole through the shingles, the felt, and the plywood, and charred the interior enough to activate the sprinklers and leave the place a mess. So the nerve center of the business moved downtown, to a building Brown now owns, on the very corner where as a boy he shined shoes.

That is, where *Mister* Brown shined shoes. They're friendly yet wonderfully cool and formal at the station, so it's Mr. Brown, Miss Moon, and Miss Tankersley. And have you met the Godfather's granddaughter, Miss Tonya Brown? Young, attractive, and dressed in good-enough-for-Sunday clothes of black, gray, and white, they're the kind of women you hope sit in your pew.

The fat guard pushes open the front door and another, fitter-looking security man enters, wearing a blue suit. He eases back his coat, revealing a pistol nesting in black leather below his left armpit. He scans the room. OK. He nods. And the Godfather of Soul walks in, looking like a million bucks.

It's April 3, a month before his sixty-eighth birthday, but James Brown looks, what, thirty? Fifty? Perhaps his timeless appearance is due to his ornately coiffed hair, which looks about the same now as when he shouted his first chart topper in 1956. Maybe it's the clothes: He's worn the same cut of colorful suits over a collarless shirt for years. Today the shirt is black silk, the necklace is big and gold, and the suit is emerald, with a raised herringbone pattern. He's got the energy to record and release a new CD, entitled *I'm Back.* There's a new single: "Killin' Is Out (School Is In)." He performed at halftime of the Super Bowl in 1997. While legal problems and a discouraging cycle of drug use and drug rehab have devalued his franchise over the years—especially in his hometown—still he's one of the first great black entertainment entrepreneurs, and beloved by black and white alike around the world. Yes, he'd be pleased to talk to you about Tigerwoods, which he pronounces as one word. Let's do it on the air, he says.

"Mixed marriage is the only kind that can work," Mr. Brown is saying. He's led you into the windowed control room, where passersby on Broad Street stop, point, and wave. He reintroduces you to his pretty, honey-voiced granddaughter, the morning DJ. "Her man is Irish. My woman is Norwegian. 'Cause you know if you can get by the race part, everything else is easy."

Michael Jackson finishes trilling "Never Can Say Goodbye," and the Hardest Working Man in Show Business takes the microphone. Other men's faces are the book of their lives, but James Brown's history is in his voice. You hear the backwoods and the big city in his raspy Georgialina growl, and concert halls and slave ships. "I didn't get into golf a lot because golf was a rich man's game and unfortunately I was poor and black," he says. "I didn't have a chance to wait for Tigerwoods. I went on and started singin' 'Please! Please! Please!' and 'Papa's Got a Brand New Bag.'

"America was not responsive to the black man when I was comin' up. But Tigerwoods' Oriental background will help him. My advice? He must keep his feet on the ground. Be tight with his mother and father. Visit all his friends. Don't look down on nobody. Don't forget the bridge that brought you here . . . I learned to thank God."

What about Tiger's—sorry, Tigerwoods'—efforts to introduce golf to the inner city? Will kids fill their idle hands with three irons and putters and put down the weapons and crack pipes?

"There were some attempts to make some golf courses predominantly black around here but that's way in the wrong direction," he says. "I don't want nothin' all black or all white. I want it to be all people."

Without directly disagreeing, Brown clearly does not see golf or the lack of it as the proper focus. Violence is the question; communication is the answer. "I'd rather see the kids walk through the red light districts in this town than through some of the neighborhoods," he says. "The most tragic thing that ever happened to this country is kids killin' kids in school. We are in bad shape any time kids are afraid to go to school. It's happened to black kids, too, not just white, although they didn't advertise it. As you go around this country talkin' to people, I'd appreciate it if you'd let them know this is very, very important."

And with that, Miss Tonya Brown puts the new James Brown single on the air. "Killin' is out/School is in/I don't think they heard ya, brother, say it again."

Brown doesn't react much to his own song—there's no sing-along, no dance step, not even a head bob. After hearing the chorus ten times, you substitute the word "golf" for "school," which leads you to realize James Brown and Tigerwoods are traveling parallel paths to the same goal. Which approach will work, and which will fail? Does hope live in golf or in music?

If Tiger's way prevails, it will be another in an unbroken series of triumphs, but Mr. Brown has lived long enough to taste defeat. At the peak of his career the Godfather sold out Yankee Stadium and at its depth he sat in a South Carolina prison for a year and a half. So his thoughts on failure are as germane as his ever-ready bromides about success.

"The danger is, don't think your career can't go under. Like a few years ago it was all about what's his name, Vernon? Norman. Greg Norman. Same thing happened to Ben Hogan and Jack Nicholson [Nicklaus]. Get him to understand how vicious this world is. Everything in this world disappears and vacates.

"Only two things can bring Tigerwoods down: God and himself. Or himself and God."

* * *

LIKE A BOOK BY JAMES MICHENER, a season on the PGA Tour needs a quarter of its length just to clear its throat. No one really cares, no result really matters until the first major, the Masters. Because of 2000, however, 2001 presented a slightly different picture. With a few exceptions, the winter warriors got little attention—unless Woods entered the battle, in which case everyone got all giddy. Television ratings doubled, tickets sold out, and the media covered him like a wetsuit. Thus, the standard ho-hum of the reawakening tour varied between slumber and thunder, according to the whim of Tiger's schedule.

In January, Johnny Miller reviewed the wreckage of the previous season with something like disgust. Woods had won nine times out of the twenty PGA Tour events he entered in 2000, and set twenty-seven significant records. His fifteen-shot victory margin at the U.S. Open at Pebble Beach, for example, was the biggest ever, for the Open or any major. He also finished the most shots under par ever at the PGA and the British Open and cumulatively, for the four major championships. Where, Miller wondered, were the other guys? "We need someone to say, I'm gonna whip Tiger," said the 1973 U.S. Open champ, now a pleasingly blunt announcer on NBC's golf telecasts. "Nobody's got the balls to do that."

But Woods doesn't always win.

Tiger not winning on the U.S. Tour in the first quarter of 2001 cooled the TV ratings a bit and threw off the know-nothing journalists who assumed a winning streak was a winning streak, football, basketball, or golf. UNIMAGINABLE CAME TRUE ON WEST COAST SWING, headlined *USA*

Today. LIST OF ODDITIES LONG. Arnold Palmer, seventy-one, shot his age. Tiger didn't win but Joe Durant did. The thirty-five-year-old former insurance salesman played the four easy courses of the five-round Bob Hope tournament in 36 under par—better than seven under per day!—to break Tom Kite's record for a five-round tournament by one shot.

It snowed at the Touchstone Energy Tucson Open, and a red-haired stranger named Garrett Willis won. A stocky second-year player from Tennessee, Willis made a Special Olympics kid's day during one of the tournament rounds when he gave him a golf ball and a howdy, but he betrayed a tendency to bloviate in the pressroom. Q: "What was it like to see your name on top of the leader board?" A: "It was pretty cool. It was something I worked for and I might not necessarily have thought it would come this soon but I got off to a pretty good start and being one of the first couple tee times out there if you can make some birdies early and post a number they post other guys with the same score beneath you because you've played more holes so I had that going for me as well." Willis said that after the third round. His blow-by-blow after he won went on and on, like a Kenny G concert.

Two weeks later, three occurrences at the Phoenix Open left 'em buzzing. First: The winner broke the Tour's forty-six-year-old record for lowest score, and he did it while holding his putter like it was a divining rod instead of a golf club. Mark Calcavecchia, forty, one of Tiger's newest and best buddies, shot a chin-dropping 65-60-64-67 for a 256 total, tying the mark for most strokes under par at 28.

He averaged 64 in part by making everything with his ergonomically incorrect "modified claw" grip, in which the palm of his right hand faced his right kneecap, not the handle of the club. But he couldn't practice his bizarre grip too much because it was so uncomfortable that after a few minutes his right wrist began to cramp.

Second: Andrew Magee made a hole in one on a par four, the first in Tour history, on the 333-yard seventeenth at the TPC at Scottsdale. The group in front of him had not cleared the green when Magee hit, and when his ball skittered up on the green it glanced off the putter belonging to Tom Byrum, who was crouched eight feet from the hole. "First putt he's made all day," caddie Tommy Uresti quipped. "I just killed it and hit it right at the flag and got a great bounce," explained Magee succinctly. And what kind of club did you use? a writer wanted to know. "A brand-new Cleveland Quad Pro, a beautiful driver," said Magee, who knows who butters his bread. "Fourty-four-inch, ninety-four-gram graphite shaft. Cleveland. Cleveland. Cleveland. Cleveland."

And third: Tiger entered but DIDN'T WIN! Just as the heretofore World's Greatest Player, Jack Nicklaus, has so far failed to win in 506 of the 576 events he's played on the U.S. Tour. More notable was that Tiger's streak of fifty-two rounds at par or better ended with his second-round 73. He hadn't ended a day in plus numbers since the impossible British Open of 1999 at Carnoustie. More remarkable still was the orange incident. On a hill above the ninth green in the first round, a fifteen-year-old boy rolled citrus on the surface as Woods attempted a birdie putt. The orange missed Tiger, and Tiger missed the hole—but he still shot 65.

The moving fruit was more a symptom of a famously exuberant gallery than an indication of negative vibes toward Woods. On the contrary, they love Tiger in Phoenix. "His first year here was in '97," recalls John Perkinson, the tournament chairman. "We just got a call from his dad about him entering. We told him how excited we were, what his presence could do for us. 'We're not doing it for you,' Earl said. 'We're doing it to win your tournament.' "

The PGA Tour in 2001 was off to a curious start. The winning scores in each of the first half-dozen events were lower than in the previous year—which may be no big deal in itself, and could be attributed to a dozen random factors working together, particularly weather. But the *amount* the scores were lower—twenty-eight shots—must mean something. Joe Durant at the Bob Hope and Calcavecchia at Phoenix had been like Russell Crowe in the Colosseum. Were they and the other gladiators answering Johnny Miller's cojones question?

A final case in this point came in February, on the last day of the AT&T National Pro-Am, when Davis Love III awoke seven shots behind the leader, Mickelson. But Tiger had won this very tournament from the same deficit the year before, and precedent can be a powerful thing. Love began his round birdie-eagle-birdie-birdie-birdie-birdie-birdie, the best seven-hole stretch in Tour history. Vijay Singh hit it in the ocean on seventeen, and Mickelson sliced a desperate driver into the big pond on eighteen.

And Love won. His 63 set a tournament record for lowest round ever in the venerable event. He acknowledged the cheers as he exited the eighteenth green, and keyed-up reporters jockeyed to get in position for an interview.

With Tiger, who'd finished eight shots back.

THE MEDICAL COLLEGE OF GEORGIA is a concrete box sitting on a concrete plain in downtown Augusta. The beds on its upper floors on the northeastern side have a soothing view of the cocoa-colored water of the Savannah River, flowing left to right, and beyond that, on the other side of the trees at the water's edge, South Carolina. On the ground floor near the parking garage there's a ten-table sandwich shop called The Sandwich Shop. Disinfectant and formaldehyde hover in the air in the corridor outside, then you push open the glass doors and smell chicken soup.

Charles Howell III and Heather Myers enter in slow lockstep, like conjoined twins. They approach to within two steps of the counter to examine the menu overhead, red letters on a white background, and even their eyes move in unison. "Turkey sandwich, I guess," Charles says softly. "What are you gonna have?"

Heather, a junior at OSU, is from Kingfisher, Oklahoma, where she played a little basketball and her mother was the coach. The Yellow Jackets, in fact, won the 2000 4A state championship. She has shoulder-length straight brown hair with subtle honey-colored highlights and the wide-eyed look of a child. Maybe you could put one over on her. But something in the way her fiancé carries himself signals that he is someone you could never fool. His is the confidence of a man who knows what he wants, whether it's the turkey on whole wheat or to whip Tiger's ass. His wire coat hanger of a body narrows to a twenty-eight-inch waist and his zero-maintenance do is an army of follicles, each one centimeter long and standing at attention. But he has mild brown eyes and an easy way with people, and the military haircut disguises a secret. As you discover from the yearbooks at the Westminster School, luxurious swoops of wavy light brown hair covered the head of the third- and fourth-grade Charles Howell, and he looked like a little Barry Manilow.

It's a cool and sunny noon on Wednesday of Masters Week. A few miles away—a world away—the usual tournament eve tradition unfolds without anyone in this hospital lunchroom. Today the lords of Augusta National close the big course at noon and have a nine-hole tournament on their jewel-like par 3 course in a cozy atmosphere of nostalgia (Sam Snead plays) and hilarity. (People drink beer and the players go for laughs. One year Ben Crenshaw and Mickelson traded clubs for one hole, and Ben made a par with Phil's lefthanded sticks. Phil chopped his ball into the water.) Afterward you might go to one or more of the scores of homes hosting a little get-together, like the famous Par 3 Par-Tee at Pete Scott's house.

But Howell is disinclined to celebrate. He doesn't drink, for one thing, and being just another Masters spectator feels to him "like the height of weirdness." This was to be the year he returned to play in and perhaps win his hometown tournament.

Like 1987 champion Larry Mize, Howell learned golf on the course across the fence from Augusta National, Augusta Country Club, which is nice but is not the National. He practiced four hours every day after school, and all day on weekends and during the summer. How many times had he rehearsed the high hook you need off the tee on the tenth at the National, and the cut seven iron that might be useful on number twelve? The fantasy became deeper and richer during the dozen or so rounds he played at the National over the years; it also became more plausible, because he and this course just seemed to click. He shot 79 on his first visit, at age ten, and a 66 on his last try, at age sixteen, the summer before he went off to Oklahoma State.

Still wrapped in the dream, he'd go back to the practice green at the Country Club and spend hours hitting the winning putt on eighteen, while an imaginary television announcer whispered and the world watched. "Here's Howell, with his surgeon's touch, he's the son of a surgeon, as you know. He learned to play only tantalizing yards from this spot. This for a 65 and the win in the Masters of 2001 . . ." Usually the voice belonged to Ben Wright, whose cultured British accent seemed just right for the moment. But neither Wright nor Howell would participate this year. So Charles would settle for listening to Heather and his mom make plans for the wedding in December, and for having lunch at the hospital with his dad.

Charles Gordon Howell, Jr., M.D., enters the sandwich shop in a whoosh of hospital air and a white lab coat.

A handsome man of fifty-three with a full head of gray hair, he smiles quickly, but then the smile is gone without a trace. "Call me Charlie," he says, but it's hard to call him Charlie. A faint S curve in his spine thrusts his head slightly forward, giving added power to his appraising blue eyes. Are you a charlatan, a bullshit artist, a waste of my time? the eyes ask. A formidable figure in the world of pediatric surgery, Dr. Howell regularly tells parents that he must invade the body of a beloved, sick child with scalpel and saw. Then he reports back to say the operation went well, or not so well. Mothers and fathers want specificity and compassion, he's found, not waffling. He gives it to them. It's what he's always given Charles. What he got from his own father . . . well, that's a different story. One Dr. Howell doesn't like to tell. An outsider may take months to piece it all together.

Like Thomas Jefferson, Charles Howell, Jr., was the son of a tobacco grower. On five hundred fertile acres in south Georgia, near Valdosta and the Florida line, the Howells raised a little cotton and a lot of the same sweet, mild "bright" leaf that Yankee soldiers swiped from warehouses on Sherman's March in 1864. The bluecoats chewed it, got hooked, and opened new and lasting markets in the industrial North. Charlie Junior helped his father plow, plant, weed, and spray America's first and greatest cash crop. The fields looked pretty when the sun glinted off the lime-green leaves, which by late summer had grown as big as elephant ears, and they fluttered and waved in the breeze. But this satisfying sight only meant more exhausting work—the harvest. Tobacco cultivation was hard, made harder for the father because he drank. Hung over and aging fast, he wanted his only son to take over the farm.

But at age sixteen and without his father's permission, Charlie began part-time work at the local hospital. Drawing blood pointed toward a way out of the tobacco fields. But Daddy didn't like it when he found out. Charlie played basketball but his father never went to a game. He graduated from high school and from Valdosta State, and his father didn't attend the ceremonies. Their bad relationship got irreparably worse on the day that Charlie announced he'd been accepted to medical school up in Augusta, and he would not be taking over the family business. The father barely spoke to his son after that. He just drank, missed another graduation, and died, on Thanksgiving Day in 1972.

Medical school, internship, and residency required ten intense years. On the long trips home to see his mother and his sister Cindy, and then back up to Augusta, Charlie Howell propped his textbooks up on the dashboard. He'd look at the road, read a line, look at the road, read a line—trying to memorize the sequence of a surgical procedure or the twenty-seven bones in the human hand.

"You know, little towns in Georgia don't produce a lot of high achievers," observes Deborah Hall Howell, the former nurse and native Augustan who is Charlie's wife and Charles's mother. She never met her father-in-law. "I think Charlie's mother—her name was Dorothy—wanted him to leave for medical school. She'd been a schoolteacher and believed in education. She was the driving force.

"Yes, I do think Charles is just like his father was as a

young man. They're both so driven and focused. But sometimes I wish Charles was a little more like Ben [the Howells' easygoing second son] and Ben was a little more like Charles."

His father had given him nothing but hard work and a hard time, but Charlie gave his son everything, including an adult's most precious commodity, his time. "I recognized an unusual potential and decided to do something," he says. He did a lot. Dr. Howell didn't play golf himself, but took it up—then dropped it when young Charles, whose voice still hadn't changed, beat him with such ridiculous ease anyone could see that Dad was just getting in the way. Then there were the long drives or flights to tournaments, the lessons with Leadbetter down in Orlando, and Ben saying at the dinner table, "Can we *please* talk about something besides golf?" So much attention and so many parental resources would spoil another kid, but Charles blossomed into a gentleman and a world-class athlete.

Not that it was smooth sailing all the way. In a hotel room at a junior tournament somewhere, a pouting Charles threw a can of Mountain Dew against a wall, breaking a picture frame. Dr. quietly asked Deborah to leave the room. The hard blue eyes blazed into the soft brown ones, law was laid down, and nothing similar ever happened again.

"I've made mistakes," Charlie says. "We've had our ups and downs. Most of the AJGA parents behave very well, but not all of them. I've seen some getting drunk in the [hotel] hot tub. Or they're overbearing, even abusive. Their egos are at stake. Mine isn't. But you can't help feeling so involved. . . . If you see him make shots over and over in practice, then you see him miss that same shot in the tournament, then miss it again. . . . You don't want anything bad to happen to your kid."

He still doesn't. As he dips a plastic spoon into a Styrofoam cup of soup, Dr. Howell thinks about an injustice perpetrated by the PGA Tour. Despite his talent, and the riches of his equipment-company contract, his son's career is in trouble. He doesn't have his card. In other words, he's getting into tournaments on his reputation, via invitations from tournament sponsors. He'd be allowed seven such exemptions for the year, and if he didn't win enough money, he'd have to find some minor-league tournaments to play in.

Charles Howell on the Hooters Tour would be like Vladimir Horowitz playing happy hour at the Holiday Inn, but it looks like a possibility. Because the sponsor's exemptions won't last much longer, and neither will the endorsement income, unless Howell breaks into the major leagues.

His unsettled life is partly the Tour's fault, the Howells agree. "It's ridiculous," says Charles. "It's the most closed shop I've ever seen," says Charlie. "They've done everything they can to hurt him. His agent [Rocky Hambric] wants to sue. At least five times PGA Tour officials have asked if we're going to."

If it went to court, *Howell* v. *PGA Tour* would hinge on the concept of detrimental reliance: Had the Tour done or said something that Charles relied on, and that later turned out not to be true? And had it cost him in some way? Well, yes. Three weeks after turning pro in July 2000, Howell had startled everyone but himself and his family by finishing third in the John Deere Classic, one shot out of a playoff for first. With the resultant check for $176,800 and adequate play the rest of the year, he finished the year 144th on the money list with a little over a quarter of a million dollars. The top 125 get the coveted card, which allows them to play almost any week they want. Those who just miss—the 126th- through 150th-ranked players—get a consolation prize, a pass into the final phase of the Tour's three-stage qualifying tournament. Or so everyone thought.

But no—the Tour changed its rule, and the same officials who'd been telling Howell, "We'll see you in the finals," now informed him he'd have to play in stage two. In ten days. Bad news, because no one wants to play in this middle tournament, which always has the most good players competing for the fewest openings. The first stage is no big deal for a top player, a mere weeding out of the eleven hundred or so entries, and everyone who makes it to the finals ends up with at least some status, even if it's only on the Tour's second tour, the Buy.com. At the end of the grueling process, forty-one players would get their cards to play in 2001.

Howell tried to get ready, his twenty-one-year-old mind muddled by the short notice, and by the implications of his just-announced engagement to Heather. Then a week before the first round of the second stage, somewhere between the belly of a 767 and a baggage carousel, someone stole his Callaway golf bag and all his clubs. It was all too much, and he didn't make it out of the second stage.

Again a golf pro without a tour, Howell spent two weeks

of early 2001 playing in Australia, and two months on the practice tee with Leadbetter. He mapped out the seven sponsor's exemptions he would accept, basing the decisions on which tournaments wanted him, where he'd played well in his abbreviated 2000 season, and where the competition was likely to be weakest. His only hope of playing more than seven events lay in winning enough money—several hundred thousand dollars, at least—to achieve a status called "temporary special membership" on the PGA Tour. There was a second possibility: If he won a tournament, his limbo state would end immediately. No one who knew Howell's mind and game considered this to be impossible.

But now the Tour seemed to be pulling another, even more infuriating switcheroo. Traditionally, anyone achieving a top ten—as Howell had with his tie for sixth at Atlanta the week before the Masters—was automatically in the field for the next open event (the Masters, of course, is an invitational). This put Howell in the Shell Houston Open, and his appearance wouldn't count against his seven sponsor's exemptions. Houston wouldn't count it as such. But, to the Howells' shock, the Tour said it would. Doesn't make sense, Charles and Charlie said, and it's unfair besides. This rule also changed, the Tour replied. Um, you're not gonna sue, are you?

"Houston, Dallas, New Orleans, John Deere, Kemper, Memorial," Howell says, touching the tips of the fingers on his left hand as he recites his next six events. Two tournaments a month for the next three months. After that, what? How was he supposed to catch Tiger if he couldn't even be in the same race?

The diners stow their trays and trash and prepare to leave. Not wanting the meal to end on a downbeat, someone asks Howell who is the most colorful player he's met in his scant half year as a touring pro. Who is different, who would people like to read about? A smile immediately wreathes his face; he doesn't have to think about this one. "Last year, there's a rain delay, I think it was at Coal Valley [the John Deere Classic]," Howell says. "I come into the locker room, soaking wet. It's only my third tournament and I don't know anybody. There's a big-screen TV, two couches with probably two dozen players sitting there, and behind the couches, at a table, sitting all by himself, Frank Lickliter. So I introduce myself. 'Mind if I sit down?' Sure, sure, he says. So we chat and Frank says, 'I like you. I'm gonna call you Bubba.'

"The sound on the TV is really low and Frank says, 'Can you hear that?' I say no. Frank says, 'Would someone turn that up, please?' No response. Again Frank says, 'Could someone please turn it up?' Nothing. So he says to me, 'Here's how you've got to handle these jerks.'

" 'WHICHEVER OF YOU FUCKING ASSHOLES HAS THE REMOTE, PICK IT UP AND USE IT.' Nobody turns around, but the guys shift around in their seats, and suddenly the volume goes way up."

You say your goodbyes to the lovely Heather, and to the impressive Dr. Howell, and say see you in Houston to Charles. But you can't help but think about the mysterious man named Lickliter.

*   *   *

THREE HOURS LATER and three miles away in a rented house in Conifer Place, a pine-shaded and azalea-splashed neighborhood not far from the Howells' house, Tiger Woods is getting dressed. He ties a Windsor knot in a pale-green-striped tie and puts on a cream-colored three-button suit coat that looks a little tight in the shoulders. What a pain in the ass: He'd rather relax the night before the Masters. Instead, he's got to go to Bell Auditorium in downtown Augusta and do what he did last year and two years before that—accept the Player of the Year Award from the Golf Writers Association of America. At least they'd agreed to give him the trophy or whatever at the beginning of the program instead of at the end. Then he could say a few words and leave. He won't have to chase rubber chicken across his plate or mingle with writers who have been drinking and might ask him something they've always wanted to ask. He gets behind the wheel of his white pearlized Cadillac courtesy car in the soft spring twilight.

After very brief preliminaries, the lights dim in the cavernous arena, and a movie screen slides down from above and behind the stage. A film montage plays of Tiger holing full shots during his glorious 2000 campaign, and holing long putts, and showing those wide, white teeth while accepting checks for $720,000. "Kryptonite" by Three Doors Down provides the musical accompaniment. Part of the chorus of the catchy rock tune goes, "If I go crazy then will you still call me Superman," with one voice singing the first words and two voices emphasizing the last three.

"Tiger's just playing incredible golf," Vijay Singh says over the music midway through the highlight tape, looking a little shell-shocked. "Bottom line, he's just beating the hell out of everybody else."

The lights come up and Golf Writers president Mike Purkey introduces the Player of the Year. Tiger moves with feline grace onto the stage, and Purkey hands him a crystal bowl on a dark wooden plinth. They shake hands and pose for photographs. Purkey has never met Woods before this moment: He's a senior editor with *Golf Magazine*, and Woods is affiliated with *Golf Digest*. Tiger puts the gewgaw on a table and walks to the mike.

"Hi," he says, grinning that megawatt grin, as relaxed as can be. And why shouldn't he be? No one in the world gets more practice talking to rooms full of writers. "Interesting," Tiger says. "If you watch the highlights, you'd think I didn't win a major. All Tour events." This is a laugh line and a not-too-subtle dig at the PGA Tour, which produced the video. The Tour owns none of the four majors but is always trying to create a fifth one.

Tiger speaks off the cuff but well, far better than he did in his meandering, deer-in-the-headlights Player of the Year remarks in 1998. He says thank you for this honor. He says his success is a product of many hours of practice—"I've worked hard to get where I'm at." And he says he's been lucky.

"For instance. I was playing well in Canada, gettin' it goin' a little, struggled for a couple of holes, then hit a shot on number eight straight right. Hit this kid right on the head on the fly, ball bounces straight up in the air back out onto the fairway, I hit it to two feet and make birdie. The kid never had a scratch on his head. It was cold out that day and he was soaking wet with sweat. Maybe because he was about three hundred pounds, five-six. Poor kid."

Something about the acoustics in Bell Auditorium muffles sound from the audience, particularly laughter. So Tiger's is the only chuckle heard at the fat kid remark, and after the jab at the PGA Tour, and during this little thrust at the writers: "I've gotten to know a lot of you here in the media over the last few years and that's been pretty neat. A lot times we as players might think the media's . . . uh . . . uh . . . [long pause, big smile] I think that about sums it up.

"But you're not too bad. You have your job and we have ours. There's mutual respect. But it's also neat to build friendships within that respect."

But many in the audience know this last thought to be patently untrue. Personality and necessity dictate that Tiger stay mostly aloof from the people who cover him. Some in the room recall how weary of each other Woods and the writers have become, each feeling that the other never rises above cliché.

In Phoenix, for example, Tiger had said, "The field we have assembled here, obviously are some of the top players in the world, and with that in mind, obviously there's going to be some great play and hopefully I can be right up there." Stop the presses.

Golf World columnist and author Tim Rosaforte blames the tension on a change in attitude—the media's, not Tiger's. "There's a different atmosphere. A generation ago, the media was more protective, and wanted to take care of Jack Nicklaus and Arnold Palmer," he says. "But as that *GQ* story proved, the climate has changed." Rosaforte's own relationship with the world's greatest golfer endured some strain because he wrote books entitled *Tiger Woods: The Makings of a Champion* and *Raising the Bar: The Championship Years of Tiger Woods.* Although both books were very positive, and with no *GQ*-ish traps, neither was authorized.

But there's something else going on between Woods and the media—intimidation. By inducing a bit of fear and awe in a guy with a pen, Tiger simplifies his life. With few hard questions, his press conferences become nearly effortless. He cows the press and fellow competitors in the same way: with his stature and achievement, and with an impossible-to-miss, don't-screw-with-me charisma. Those doe eyes become hooded and scary when he is displeased. No one wants to see them, so a lot of questions don't get asked. "Do you have a gambling problem? You seemed to really lose your temper on number fourteen today—does anger indicate a loss of self-control? You have a reputation of being frugal to the point of cheapness—true?"

Tough questions are perceived by Team Tiger as attacks instead of opportunities to set the record straight, and those who ask them get cut off. "You're burning bridges," IMG agent Mark Steinberg told Jaime Diaz, who dared to write something in *Sports Illustrated* that was not fawning. "What bridges?" Diaz asked.

Early in the year, ESPN's Jimmy Roberts was doing a live interview with an unhappy-looking Tiger, who answered a question or two then deliberately embarrassed Roberts by abruptly walking away—apparent payback for Roberts's earlier reference to Tiger's "slump."

Inspired by Woods's white lie about his burgeoning friendships in the media and by the presence of the LPGA Player of the Year, Karrie Webb, whose relationship with writers is lower than whale shit, a discussion erupts as the banquet lights come up and Tiger leaves.

Marino Paracenzo, a veteran writer from Pittsburgh, recalls the time 1996 PGA champion Mark Brooks agreed, reluctantly, to an interview—then would only speak in the roped-off runway between some eighteenth green and the locker room. The writer asked a question and Brooks answered, but started to walk—faster and faster, it seemed to Paracenzo, who weighs a few cannolis more than Brooks's 150 pounds. Like Secretariat at Belmont, Brooks built his lead to the point that the questions had to be shouted, and the replies sounded increasingly faint. A few more paces, and Brooks disappeared without another word into the inner sanctum.

Webb walks past on her way to the buffet line. She's got her sandy blonde hair down, looking relaxed in a dark pantsuit. A *Golf Magazine* writer recalls the time in May 2000 when he was sent to interview Ms. Webb, and she displayed body language even more negative and insulting than Brooks's fast walk. Although she'd agreed to the interview, Webb indicated her displeasure with the first question or with the reporter's deodorant or with life itself by employing a singularly eloquent gesture: she turned her back on the flabbergasted reporter. After a bit of maneuvering to look into her eyes, and a second implied invitation to talk to her butt, the writer waited for his target on the practice tee. Maybe he could stand behind her, and at least address questions to the champ in profile? No. "She wants you to go away," her caddie said after a few minutes.

Someone recalls the U.S. Amateur at Champions Golf Club in Houston in 1993 when a sixteen-year-old Tiger stiffed the USGA's writer for an interview then blew off the USGA's photographer for a scheduled shoot. "That's when I knew he was gonna be big," photographer Robert Walker said later, more amused than amazed. "He was already acting like a superstar."

Others around the room have their stories. "Well, Karrie's on everyone's list," says John Garrity of *Sports Illustrated.* "I just try not to worsen my relationship with her. . . . My favorites tend to be journeymen. Scott Dunlap, or Brad Bryant, who talks to you like you're the most important person on earth. Of the bigger guys, Phil Mickelson—everyone thinks he's a phony, but he relates to me as a real person. I saw him be charming to an autograph seeker when he had every reason not to be. I hate to see him get zinged.

"Payne Stewart gave me the hardest time. I had to interview him after he missed the cut by one at the Western Open, and he's practically knocking down children on his way to the locker room. 'No way,' he says. 'You've got to be kidding.' Azinger used to be delightful. Now he won't return your calls or acknowledge your existence. Someone's advised him to shut down. He's taking on Payne's properties."

Garrity put together one of the first and one of the best of the Tiger books, a compilation of his own lucid writing and that of other *SI* staffers called *Tiger Woods: The Making of a Champion*. Which has naturally led to people asking him at the grocery store and the post office and at cocktail parties: What is Tiger like?

"I tell them I just don't know," says Garrity, a tall, impassive man who as a tall, impassive kid played bass in several rock bands. "Tiger's drawn a curtain across his personal, private life. He's so totally focused he has no empathy for others—if you're in his field of vision he looks like he's never seen you before. But I don't fault him. If he said yes to even 10 percent of us, he'd have no time to do what he does. And he's professional enough to at least do the press conferences. He doesn't want to be perceived as a prick."

Most professional golfers understand how perception and reality are two different things. The worst reprobates and the most arrogant scoundrels can paint themselves as angels on earth, simply by availing themselves of the greatest free publicity machine ever devised, the U.S. sports media. But some players can think no farther ahead than the end of the day. Everything's a transaction for them: can doing this interview help me shoot a lower score tomorrow? Or get me a higher fee for the logo on my hat? No? Then screw it. Perhaps the long-term value of name repetition and name recognition is too subtle a concept for them to grasp. Yet they only have to look at the names of the tournaments they play in to see how much the real world values a mention in the credible press. It ain't the Accenture Match Play Championship for nothing.

Still, says best-selling author and columnist John Feinstein, "Compared to baseball, football, and the NBA, there just aren't that many bad guys in golf. When I first came out, Payne [the late Payne Stewart] was just that, a pain, but he improved a lot. Nick Faldo will only give you birdies and bogies. Colin Montgomerie in a good mood is a really bright guy, he's just too seldom in a good mood. Come to think of it, the foreign guys, very generally, are harder to deal with. Frank Nobilo [a New Zealander] says to me, 'Talk to my agent.' That's death. That's what the players do in tennis."

Feinstein got plenty of the agent brushoff when he wrote a book called *The Second Coming: Tiger Woods: Master or Martyr?* "I find him very dynamic on the golf course, but not off it," Feinstein says. "Tiger gives you that big smile and ten minutes and you look down and there's nothing in your notebook. I'm very impressed with his skill—and it is a skill—at saying nothing. But the TV guys love it. A few usable words and that smile is enough for them."

The Player of the Year's effect on the daily deadline media is deep and wide but simple to summarize: You've got to keep track of Tiger. "He is *always* the story," says Lance Barrow, who produces CBS TV's golf broadcasts. "If he's winning, of course; if he's not, people want to know why not. He's taken golf from page four or five of the sports section to the front page of the paper. . . . We used to say that if you have Greg Norman and John Daly and anyone else, you've got a good tournament. Now, all you need is Tiger."

For the magazines, all you need is Tiger on the cover. Each year since 1997, when the relationship began, *Golf Digest* has regularly and sensibly played its trump card.

Because of the doctrine of fair use—because Tiger is a celebrity—any rag can use an image of Woods without compensation or permission. Even *Golf Magazine, Golf Digest's* main competitor, puts his face on its face, without fear that by doing so it somehow promotes its rival. Because while Tiger may be an effective endorser, his image is so powerful it stands apart from the trading cards, credit cards, cars, and magazines he's paid to say he likes.

Perceiving that the young, hip man dominating golf had attracted a similarly cool demographic to the game, several publishing entrepreneurs had the same brainstorm: a new golf magazine for this new audience. We'll be irreverent, they told potential investors and advertisers. Gonna kick *Golf Digest's* and *Golf Magazine's* ass. We'll have sharp reporting, a wry, ironic tone, and no more two-thousand-word Valentines about Senior Tour pros with beer guts. We won't tell you for the one-thousandth time how to beat that slice, they said, or how to stop three-putting, or how to start getting your swing into the Q Zone. We won't show you how-to anything—unless it's how to dress for golf without looking like your dad.

Three new titles gathered the resources to publish in the new Tiger-inspired genre. *Schwing!* was a dated in-word from TV's *Saturday Night Live* a decade ago, but it sounds like what you do with a golf club, and *SNL* was cool, so there you go. *Fringe Golf,* so it said, would be "ground zero for the modern golfer." The third entry figured to be the most serious player. Its publisher and point man would be Michael Caruso, formerly on the business side at *The New Yorker* and *Vanity Fair.* A persuasive, charming man with French cuffs and a quick smile, Caruso pitched the idea to various media companies, and the best possible one bit: Newscorp, Australian billionaire Rupert Murdoch's company. Newscorp publishes *USA Today* and owns the Fox TV Network, but it had never had a magazine. *Maximum Golf* would be its first. Caruso assembled an experienced staff with Murdoch's money and put them on the twelfth floor of the giant media conglomerate's building on Avenue of the Americas in Midtown Manhattan. He also had an artificial turf practice green installed in the office, and you wonder if he had a hard time sneaking that expense past accounting.

"Unlike any golf magazine you've ever seen," read the come-on to new subscribers. "*Maximum Golf* is the only magazine that captures the new spirit of golf. Inside dirt on young pros like Sergio, Duval . . . and that Tiger guy." The first issues held a number of surprises, including a liberal use of the word "freaking" as an adjective, imaginative graphics, and a cart girl of the month. The cart girls—attractive young on-course beverage dispensers from around the country—wore short shorts and tight freaking tops.

The banquet concludes and the lights come up again. Several *Maximum Golf* staffers become visible, arguing with their presence that their new magazine is legit. But an editor from *Golf Magazine* eyes a colleague's nametag on which is written his new affiliation with the cart girl periodical. "When you lie down with swine," the editor says grimly, and walks away.

* * *

THE SEVEN-THIRTY COLD on Thursday morning grips you between the shoulder blades and cramps your neck. The sunlit dew glitters too brightly the morning after the night before, and too many people are trying to worm their way into too small a place. It would look like hell, but the first tee at Augusta National needs a grandstand. At least it does for the few minutes required for one of the Masters' most charming traditions, the ceremonial tee shots that begin the tournament.

The three elders starring in this year's performance of the long-running play must be feeling the chill, too, but only one of them looks uncomfortable. Byron Nelson has been dreading this moment for months. He's eighty-nine, and the hips are gone—replaced with titanium, and a bother ever since. He's got nerve damage in his right ankle, making his stride still more painful and tentative, and his left leg *really* hurts. He's getting around with a cane in his right hand and his wife Peggy's hand in his left, but he plainly needs a walker. This shot, and practice for this shot, is about the extent of his golf nowadays. Byron tells you that he's hit exactly eight shots since last September. That is, until yesterday, when he whacked at twenty balls on the practice tee at Augusta Country Club. This will be his last shot in public.

Next to Byron stands Sam Snead, one-third of the proof that 1912 was golf's best year; Nelson was born in February, Snead in May, and the late Ben Hogan in August. Snead is gimpy, too, but his joints seem wondrously lubricated, and he can still swing.

The third man on the tee wears glasses, a happy-tobursting look, and the green coat of the Augusta National inner circle. A square-jawed man with a full head of extremely brown hair despite his sixty-nine years, he's got a South Ca-lina accent as full of grits as his nickname. He grips a microphone, not a driver, for he's the emcee of this ceremony and a member of the club. But he's not just any member; he is the chairman. And he's not just any chairman. Someday, William Woodward "Hootie" Johnson, retired banking entrepreneur, will be remembered as either the best—or the worst—chairman in the club's seventy-year history. Without question, he's the most daring.

Certainly none of the other four previous occupants of the throne effected so much change in so short a time. No one's even close. Since his surprising elevation in May 1998—most outsiders expected Jack Stephens to be succeeded by another charmer from Arkansas, Joe Ford—Johnson caused or at least approved five fundamental changes in the course and the tournament. Not that he'd admit it, but Hootie and his cabinet had Woods in mind for four of them.

"Tiger is an outstanding golfer, and a wonderfully conditioned athlete and in the forefront of today's great young players," says Johnson, who responds to questions via Glenn Greenspan, the Masters media man. "However, we do not make changes because of one player or one tournament."

Yet when Tiger laughed at par in 1997—winning by twelve shots at 18 under, the lowest Masters score ever—Johnson and the other members were deeply offended. What would be next? Twenty under? Had the Masters devolved into the Bob Hope Chrysler Classic? Perceiving that certain players were not getting their just deserts for extremely long but inaccurate driving, the chairman directed Augusta National superintendent Billy Owen to do something to the fairway mowers that had never been done—raise them. And in 1999 Augusta National had rough for the first time in its life. Which neither the architect nor his advisor—Alister MacKenzie and Bobby Jones—had wanted. Which the members hate. And which the club calls "the second cut," a boring euphemism it forces the TV announcers to use.

A second change in the Johnson administration had little or nothing to do with Tiger. As a response to criticism that Masters fields had fewer quality players than many PGA Tour events, qualification criteria were made very close to those in . . . a PGA Tour event.

But you couldn't miss Tiger's influence when Hootie broke with tradition and announced the amount and the recipient of the club's donation to charity. Spurred by the desire to give something back and by the tax laws, Augusta National had for years been giving away some of its excess profits. But no one knew who got the cash or how much cash, until Mr. Johnson announced a $3-million donation in 1999 to a cause identified with Tiger—the First Tee. The karmic value of anonymous giving lost out to the undeniable public-relations benefit of letting the world know that Augusta National wanted to help inner-city youth get into golf. "I did decide on the giving, that it should go public," Hootie said. "I don't see where that policy of not letting people know what we were doing was good."

Chairman Johnson denied that Tiger had anything to do with going public regarding its donations to good causes, which are now over $10 million in the last four years. That the money went to the First Tee was largely the outgoing chairman's idea. Jack Stephens had investigated building a golf facility for poor kids in Little Rock, his hometown, after Tiger won the Masters in 1997, and before the First Tee was announced. Stephens, Hootie's partner in club competitions at Augusta National, donated $5 million to the organization.

A fourth change regarding television coverage related in part to Tiger's overwhelming popularity. The club would now allow TV to show the first five holes, none of which the stay-at-home Masters fan had ever seen. Masters coverage in recent years had crept slowly backward, all the way to the sixth hole—but beginning in 2002, CBS on the weekend and USA on Thursday and Friday would show all eighteen. Why accede now to television's perennial request to show more and show it longer? It must have something to do with the unprecedented ratings achieved during the Tiger era. Two hours of air were added to the Masters show on CBS on the weekend, thirty minutes on Saturday, and at least ninety minutes on Sunday. Add the impact of two new TV sponsors—IBM and Coca-Cola, replacing Cadillac—and add the qualification changes, the rough, and the new policy regarding its charitable donations, and Mr. Johnson had changed things more in thirty-six months than his three predecessors had in twenty-six years. Only Cliff Roberts, the original chairman and the cofounder of the club and the tournament, did more to mold the Masters.

Tiger had a hand in a final profound change at the Masters. No one can identify the exact moment when the guardians of par at Augusta National got really sick of what Woods was doing in 1997—perhaps it was when he hit a hard eight iron for his second shot on the par 5 fifteenth hole, and the ball flew laughing over the pond and past the flagstick. Tiger, titanium, and the Surlyn-covered golf ball had emasculated the damn hole—maybe all he'd needed was a nine. The fifteenth had been a great par 5 back when a player had a go or no-go decision. Who could forget the excitement when Arnie stood in the fairway, his hands on his hips, squinting at the hole through his own cigarette smoke. Finally, the internal debate settled—Palmer didn't consult his homegrown caddie, Ironman, at such times—with the air of a gambler pushing all his chips into the pot, the strongest player of his day . . . took the cover off his three wood! He's goin' for it! People told each other in delicious anticipation. But where was the drama—and the challenge—when the strategic decision now lay in choosing between this short iron and that one?

Johnson's in a tough battle, and he knows it. The very game is at stake. "Of course, we've added some distance," the chairman says. "The ball and the equipment have made this imperative. As I recall, Freddie Couples hit a seven iron on number eighteen when he won in 1992, and he hit a sand wedge to a pitching wedge four days this year. Obviously, something had to be done."

Soon after the last putt was holed in 1998, the bulldozers and workers and architect Tom Fazio rolled onto

Augusta National. A major lengthening and toughening ensued, with substantial changes to four holes. But with the tournament on the line on the last hole of the final round in 1999, Tiger drove it around the trees and so far up the hill he had a mere half sand wedge to the green. Had it been only fifteen years since Greg Norman, the strongest player of his day, famously misplayed his *four-iron* second shot to eighteen on Sunday? Obviously, the equipment manufacturers and Tiger were embarrassing Augusta National. On Wednesday, the day before this Masters, Chairman Johnson announced soberly that it was time to build again.

But that was yesterday. Now in the Thursday-morning chill, Hootie Johnson clears his throat. "Ladies and gentlemen, the winner of eleven consecutive tuna-mints, eighteen in one year, and two times Masters champion, Lord Byron Nelson!" Nelson, who hasn't liked the reference to the famous poet ever since he discovered that the original Lord Byron had a club foot and lived a rather scandalous life, hobbles up to the plate. As she's done in recent years, Byron's wife, Peggy, has teed one up for him. "OK, little ball, one more time," he says, and makes a game swipe and pretty good contact. Everyone cheers. He leaves his tee in the ground. Then Snead swings his timeless swing, which age has abbreviated by about a quarter. Sam picks up his tee and grins. "Let the tuna-mint begin!" the chairman calls out over the applause. The past has been saluted, and the Masters has begun.

* * *

LATER YOU WALK OVER to the practice range, the sharp smell of cedar chips and pine straw in your nostrils—it's been wet, and they sprinkle the aromatic burnt-orange mixture on the mud in the high-traffic areas. Jack Nicklaus enters the tee, looking his sixty-one. Then Tiger enters, Superman in plain clothes, wearing banker's gray on the increasingly gray day, and large white swooshes, one on the hat, one on the chest. Nicklaus gives the boy-king a nod and a wink as he walks past. Tiger points at the ground ten steps behind Jack, and there caddie Steve Williams puts down the big black Buick bag. Instructor Butch Harmon stands a few paces behind his student, impassive, silent, chewing gum, wearing shades, and looking for God-knows-what in that godlike swing.

At one point, Nicklaus and Woods strike a few times in unison, Jack with his driver, Eldrick with the two iron. Their shots travel identical distances, both balls one-hopping into the net at the end of the range.

When Tiger completes his exertions, the crowd gives him a perfectly ridiculous standing ovation. A standing, walking ovation, because almost everyone leaves the area when Woods, Williams, and Harmon march off, stage right.

Thursday settles nothing, of course, but it confirms what regular Masters watchers know in their bones: Tiger has inherited Arnie's gallery, the least knowledgeable and most enthusiastic fans. Augusta National is as always a collection of partially enclosed theaters, and the audience in any one can hear the applause and group groans in any other. Augusta National's membership is getting younger, they say, but the members you see remain a vision of green (coat), yellow (tie), gray (hair), and pink (face). The concessions staff still treats you like a king just because you buy a cup of coffee. "No, I'm not getting tired," says the woman behind the counter, pouring her one-thousandth cup. "People are so happy to get their coffee it just makes me glad." The course is still green velvet and pink blossoms. Byron still sits behind the first tee and shakes the nervous right hand of every man before he begins his battle. This comforting sameness overlaid by white-hot competition is a seductive combination, like a beautiful woman in blue jeans and a silk blouse.

Tiger shoots 70, and trails Chris DiMarco and Angel Cabrera, among others, two guys with musical names and big golf games.

On Friday you enter Augusta National with a heavy heart, because an unusually enthusiastic mood killer is operating opposite the main gates on Washington Road. "The Lord said you MUST be born again, not you MAY be born again," shouts the knit-browed street-corner preacher. He's a type: white man of about forty, with a short-sleeved white shirt, a skinny black tie, hair cut to the quick. "The wages of SIN is DEATH! You are DESTROYING your immortal souls when you don't declare your faith in Jesus Christ Our Lord. 'For all have sinned and come short of the glory of God. . . .' " People avert their eyes lest one of the man's young children put a pamphlet in their hands, and they cross the road quickly when the light changes, pretending not to hear the harangue. But the preacher goes on all week.

You arrive at the practice tee as a priest begins to hit balls. No wait—it's just golf's very own ascetic, David Robert Duval, in head-to-toe black and dark, dark wraparound shades. If he were a holy man, Duval would be a Jesuit, the Catholic sect known for its reverence for intelligence and learning. He's a reader, a skeptic, a parser of sentences, and so unemotional it's easier to read the face of Father John on the other side of the confessional. No one chasing Tiger is closer to catching him, except, perhaps, Mickelson. Although Duval's interruption of Tiger's reign at the top of the World Golf Rankings was brief, it inspired a pitiful hope among the scribblers that he will deliver soliloquies about the pressures and pleasures of life at the top. But writers seldom get great answers from him because they seldom ask great questions. He simply doesn't answer inquiries he considers too personal or too stupid, and other questions don't get a real reply because he won't concede the premise behind them. His pretournament press conference produced these examples of unclear communication:

Q: Any kind of trepidation this week? (Duval had been out for the three weeks before the Masters with a wrist injury.)

A: I don't know. That's kind of like when you're asked "How important is it for you?" I mean, how do you quantify it?

Q: Were you glad there were no significant changes made to the course this year?

A: Was I glad?

Q: Is that fine with you . . .

A: Again, they have still failed to call me when they are thinking about changes here . . . I feel like it's kind of a waste of time for the players to talk if they would like changes or not because there's nothing they can do about it. It's not up to them. It's just there to play.

Q: Your game, of all the majors seems best suited for, I would think, a U.S. Open?

A: Thank you.

A feature story in *Sports Illustrated* intimated he is the way he is because of two wrenching experiences in his childhood, his parents' divorce and the death from cancer of his brother, for whom he donated bone marrow in a series of painful procedures involving a very large syringe. Nope, Duval said, lots of people endure tragedy, and writers shouldn't presume there's an automatic link between incidents from childhood and the arc of an adult's life.

Whatever the cause, talent and discipline coalesced within him. He won four tournaments in 1999, briefly breaking Tiger's stranglehold on the top of the world rankings, then showed up for the first tournament of 2000 with a new body—he'd been slightly pudgy before—and varied the configuration of the hair on his head and on his face. Now he looked as sleek and strong as Lance Armstrong. How much weight did you lose, David? a writer asked. "I didn't keep track," Duval said. Tell us about the new diet? "I did not go on a diet." Then how . . . ? "I've worked very hard lifting weights and running and eating very well . . . if there's a secret, it's in working hard."

Did he have a particular face or name in mind as he ran this grueling race? No. "I want to become a better player and I want to improve," Duval said. "If it's to beat Tiger, then so be it." Some doubted a man so driven could run in second place and block out the identity of the man in first.

Yet on Friday Duval shows a remarkable ability to focus on the waltz in his head while a hip-hop boom box blasts nearby. Self-controlled and self-contained, he shoots 66, while his playing partners allow themselves to become furious at this infuriating golf course. One of them, Colin Montgomerie, three-putts the roller-coaster eighth green, making bogey on a birdie hole. On nine, a forecaddie in a white jumpsuit blithely walks behind him as he addresses his difficult second shot, 160 years uphill, from a sidehill lie, and over a Sahara of dazzling white sand. Monte backs away from the shot and sings out, in polite but firm Scottish accents, "EXCUSEMEHOLDSTILLPLEASETHANKYOU." Then he hits his iron too hard, to the back fringe, and again, he three-putts. Boiling now, the blush on his face forms a vivid contrast between his blond hair and his robin's-egg-blue shirt. He pull-hooks his tee ball on ten into the woods. Tries to chip out but the ball gets tangled in pine straw and Augusta rough. "For fuck's sake, don't stop now!" he calls in rage and despair. His third shot's a low bullet to the right of the green, leaving an impossible pitch over a bunker to a tight pin. He pitches it in the sand. Hits it on to four feet. Lips out the putt. Triple bogey seven.

The third member of the threesome, a pro from Denver named Jonathan Kaye, also has his troubles on ten. When his shortish second putt hangs on the lip, he gives the ball the finger.

In the midst of this bad golf and anger, Duval hits his ball from the middle of the tenth tee to the middle of the fairway to the middle of the green and just misses from eighteen feet for a birdie.

Chris DiMarco leads at day's end with 65-69—134. Waiting with all the patience of the next guy in line at a pay phone are Woods and the scrub-faced Mickelson, two shots back. Father David and Calcavecchia will begin round three three back.

Saturday: Despite the aficiando's dream of a leader board, and sunshine, Tigermania seems muted. "I've been able to shoot from places I haven't been able to get to in years," says photographer Fred Vuich. This week groups of thirty and forty with reserved starting times at nearby Jones Creek CC have simply not showed up. "Goll, it was a lot busier last year," says bottled-water seller Lelia Sakata, one of the entrepreneurs on Washington Road. "I think it's the economy," says Augusta stockbroker Kathy Starrett. "Plus everyone knows Tiger's gonna win."

Ken Venturi, the former U.S. Open champion who has helped refine the games of a number of Tour players, meets Chris DiMarco at the locker-room door. Time for a pep talk: DiMarco's paired with Tiger today. Venturi puts his hands on the younger man's shoulders. "What got you there is gonna bring you there," he says mysteriously.

Not pulling into Magnolia Lane are three guys who

could add some magic to the day, Gary Player, Nicklaus, and Palmer. They'd been paired together Thursday and Friday, forming a concentrated blast of nostalgia for an event that surely already has enough. A great deal of the Augusta National gallery plunks down lawn chairs and parks for the day like RVs at certain holes, especially on the back nine, and these people felt compelled to give the threesome a standing ovation each time they approached. But this ignored the fact that all three men are still competitive, even though they are not the competitors they once were. For the first time in their lives, they're getting applause after bogies. They're being patronized but they pretend not to mind.

There was Arnie on thirteen on Friday, fighting like hell to break 80. He fumbled around through the green and with his fourth shot got the ball on the top shelf, no-man's-land, and had to putt back down the icy slope. The ball would not go in—he five-putted. Nostrils flared and color creeping up his neck, he trudged to the fourteenth tee—where the crowd rose as one and cheered. Palmer forced a smile that was almost a grimace, then took his driver out of the bag and stood to the side of the tee. He bowed his head and looked at nothing.

Months later, Oprah would ask Tiger about his dream foursome. He picked Jack, Hogan, and Jones, each in his prime, the clear implication being that these were and are the best four ever. They'd each play the same equipment and they'd just see who came out on top. But there are other candidates for best in show. Two men whose records Tiger has not yet exceeded are Gary Jack Player and Arnold

Daniel Palmer. And Palmer in his prime might beat all of them, simply because he recovered so brilliantly from trouble and made so many long putts he demoralized his opposition.

Like Arnie, Tiger putts like he invented putting, but it's the least appreciated aspect of his game. Where he causes creeping hopelessness in his opponents is his strength, his length. "Where he's hitting sand wedge, I'm hitting seven iron," says DiMarco in the Saturday postgame. "I don't know what he hit into the par 5s [on the back nine], but it couldn't have been more than seven iron." Actually, he didn't need that much. On thirteen, Tiger had about 185 to the hole on the par 5 after he'd absolutely crushed his tee shot. His eight iron carried 190 yards, safely onto the green.

Both Duval and Mickelson salute their rival in their postround remarks by referring to him simply as he—or He. "It's just up to me," Duval says. "I can't be real concerned about what he is doing or anybody else." Duval would start the final round three back.

"I desperately want this, very much so," Mickelson says. Like Duval, he's never won a major, mostly because of Him. "I've been preparing for this not just the last year or the last ten years but since I was a little kid picking up practice balls at a driving range so I could practice as much as I needed to."

Mickelson is pleased to have birdied the final two holes on Saturday, which pulls him into solo second a shot behind the leader. They would be paired together on Sunday. "I want to be playing with him and know where we stand," Phil says.

Earl Woods has arrived on the scene, although he can't walk the course. Colon cancer and diabetes have been added to his medical chart, just below the heart and weight problems. But as ever, Tiger will take strength from his father into the final round.

On Sunday, DiMarco and Cabrera fade away. Calcavecchia's run ends on thirteen. In the fourth round in 1992, he'd birdied in from this hole. Three back and desperate, he needs another string of miracles. His left-to-right ball flight is as ingrained as his thumbprint, but the opposite spin helps on thirteen, so he goes for it. Calc overcooks the hook, however, and the ball darts into the shaded, rocky creek left of the fairway. The three best players in the world will decide the thing.

Duval is unbelievable. After ten holes he has one par, two bogies, *seven* birdies, and a tie for the lead with Woods. He's strategizing brilliantly, and sinking difficult putts unemotionally. With the pinch between his cheek and gum and his hidden eyes, he looks like a poker player you just can't beat. But is he bluffing?

Meanwhile, a hole behind Duval, Woods is emoting enough for three men. Television and most fans love this about him, of course, just as they're plainly unenthusiastic about Duval's level of emotional sharing (Mickelson is somewhere in the middle). If Tiger has a flaw as a sportsman, it's the extravagance of his gestures, which could easily disturb a fellow competitor's concentration. His "take that!" fist pumps after made putts clearly incite his audience. But today Tiger holes putts tougher than Chinese algebra on seven, eight, nine, and ten and then sticks an eight iron to ten inches on eleven and he looks only faintly pleased. Today his grandest emoting expresses not joy but disappointment on a cosmic, why-hast-thou-forsaken-me scale. Putts that just miss on thirteen, fourteen, and sixteen cause the full head-back, eyes-closed reaction, followed by despairing hands to the face. The club falls from his hands and over his shoulder when a chip refuses to go in on seventeen. Mickelson would say later that he didn't notice any of this. But the mere fact that a player so good communicates so vividly that he is trying *extremely* hard, maybe harder than you, is an important component of Tiger's psychological warfare. Only once has anyone played really well when paired with Woods in the last round of a major—Bob May at the PGA in 2000.

Mickelson hangs in, but he cannot sustain a rally. Missing at least half a dozen putts from inside four feet during the last two rounds, including a very damaging three-putt on sixteen, Phil shoots 70 the last day and finishes tied for third. In the midst of all those misses, he has a bushel of makes: He breaks Jose Maria Olázàbal's record for birdies. Like Greg Norman, Mickelson seems to have only one style—high-risk—and one speed—flat-out. Maybe he's the mysterious one, not Duval. In the end, Phil probably should have won.

Duval stands on the sixteenth tee tied for the lead. He selects a club and swings. A player of his caliber hits solid shots all the time, but this seven iron is something special, so purely struck and on such a perfect line that later he said, "It might be the best golf shot I ever hit . . . to be perfectly honest, I thought I might have made a one."

He made a four. The odd intersection of force and physics results in a shot that is *too* good. "I really don't have an explanation for it," Duval would say half an hour later. "It's 183 yards and I hit seven iron and flew it over the green."

He hits two more perfect iron shots on the last two holes, giving him in effect two more chances to win the Masters. But his putter has iced over and he misses both eight-footers. As usual, his postmortem comments contain more honesty than you'd expect and less contrition. "I probably just pulled it a little bit," he says of the putt on eighteen. "I missed. I knew I needed to make it. I'm very proud of how I played and the golf shots I hit."

Duval has shot a 67, which could easily have been lower. He probably should have won, too.

Woods had heard the roar from the eighteenth green when Duval hit it close. He had a one-shot lead—which he assumes will be a none-shot lead after Duval makes his birdie putt. This is when Tiger hits the howitzer drive that cements in the minds of Hootie Johnson and the others that their golf course is too short. Woods walks up the eighteenth fairway seeing only the shadows on the dark green grass on the steep hill in front of him. The sun hits him in the face as he crests the hill, then the top of the clubhouse becomes visible, and the people and the cameras and the scoreboard, which confirms that Duval has missed. He still has a one-shot lead, and the simplest of shots to the green, a wee pitch from eighty yards. The drama is gone now but the power of the moment remains.

Tiger bunts it up about five steps past the hole. Behind the green his parents stand beaming, applauding with thousands of others for their son. He needs only two putts to become the first golfer ever to hold the four major championships concurrently. Just two putts.

He needs only one.

3

CHASING FRANK LICKLITER

> Sportswriters . . . have a tendency to believe that the most telling aspect of any athlete's character is the way in which that athlete treats sportswriters.
>
> —David Owen, *The Chosen One*

The little jet is a flying limousine, a quiet cocoon of carpet, leather, and polished wood. It is waiting, spotless and white, its tanks topped, its flight plan filed, its two pilots rested and ready. Finally, its reason for being arrives, wearing expensive sunglasses and Nike running shoes.

Everything happens quickly. The passenger slides out of the car seat and says "bye" to one driver and "hi" to the next. He walks perhaps ten yards, up three steps, ducks through the door, snags a soft drink from a cooler, and sinks into a recliner. Someone else handles the bags. The engines start to whine, the cargo and passenger doors click shut, and then there's movement. Like a thoroughbred walking into the starting gate, the sleek machine rolls slowly into takeoff position. A couple of minutes later it's doing five hundred miles per hour, going from Augusta to Orlando, taking Tiger home.

The passenger feels like hell. Released from the stress of winning his fourth consecutive major, and talking about it, and smiling as the guest of honor at the traditional dinner in the Augusta National clubhouse after all the public ceremony, his body rebels at all it's been through. His temperature spikes to 102 degrees. Back home in his mansion behind the gates of Isleworth in suburban Orlando, Woods stays in bed with his flu for four days. At this odd moment—now officially the king of the world, but sick as a dog—he gets just what he needs from the telephone. His mother calls from Tustin with comfort—"Go get some chicken soup," she says—and his father calls from Cypress with love and inspiration. "We talked for about an hour," Tiger says later. "It was just really neat to talk to my dad like that. . . . We talked mostly about Augusta and what it meant to me to have him there."

He takes the next twenty-nine days off. His downtime seems half-purposeful and half-not, combining video games, music, junk food, and rest—Tiger's a champion sleeper—with hours on the practice tee. There are also some eighteen-hole strolls with his neighbors, fellow PGA Tour players John Cook and Mark O'Meara. All three wear shorts, ride carts, and compete like the devil in these "casual" matches. Woods also makes and takes innumerable business e-mails and phone calls during his hiatus, but mostly he's just getting away. Like the other megacelebrities from recent generations—the Beatles and Michael

Jordan come to mind—he's obsessed with privacy because autograph hunters and run-of-the-mill idolaters are obsessed with invading it. They would steal his life if he let them, and the media would take what the others missed. The jet satisfies his human desire to be left alone from time to time, as does his interest in self-contained underwater breathing apparatus. In the air with his window seat or under the sea with his scuba, Woods can be a spectator himself for a change, instead of the big fish under glass.

Only one thing can get him to break cover during his post-Masters hiatus—the Tiger Woods Foundation. Twice he charms the kids and fixes their backswings at Coca-Cola/Tiger Woods Foundation Junior Golf Clinics. With his voice amplified from a microphone clipped onto his collar, Tiger answers questions and comments on shots he's just hit, and his patter is as smooth as his swing. "The problem with stepping on one, and cranking up the juice a little bit, is that it's hard to keep the ball accurate," he'll say, referring to the difficulties of taking a really hard cut with a driver. "So now I'll crank one up a little bit and you will notice immediately the difference in the speed of the ball . . ." The ball sings off the titanium—*threek*—and a bleacherful of kids will breathe, "Oh, wow."

"The most memorable aspect of Tiger's visit was his spirit," said Dr. Tommy Dorsey of the Orlando Minority Youth Golf Association after one of Tiger's Coca-Cola Clinics. "It was so good, it was almost as if God was in the children's midst. The clinic was entertaining, informative, harmonious, joyous—all the words of goodness."

Tiger blows 'em away at his four annual Coca-Cola clinics, often with Earl's help as cohost. But driver demonstrations for overawed city kids can only go so far—they know they're seeing something great, but they don't have enough grounding to know how great. Raising up the lowest and the poorest is fine but it's so Al Gore; inspiring already motivated kids to go still higher is an equally worthy goal and fits Tiger's politics and his personality much better. Thus, the Tiger Woods Foundation organizes all-star teams to compete against each other. One day one of his kids will win the Open, and Tiger will have made another indelible mark.

At the end of April he's back in the jet, bound for Sin City, where he hosts Tiger Jam IV presented by Coca-Cola, a concert to benefit the Tiger Woods Foundation. Featured jammers at the Mandalay Events Center in Las Vegas are Third Eye Blind and John Mellencamp, succeeding the blondes of Tiger Jam III, Christina Aguilera and Lee Ann Rimes. Tickets start at forty-five dollars, and ten thousand attend. Tiger goes onstage between acts and says a few words, his black shirt and black leather jacket absorbing the spotlight.

"[He] went onstage and said the band was awesome," wrote Doug Elfman of the *Las Vegas Review-Journal* the next day. "[But] I met Woods earlier backstage and he didn't seem like such a music fanatic." The writer asked the golfer if he sang on the golf course. No. In the car? No. In the shower? No. Why did you choose these particular bands? "They said yes," Tiger said. "It was that simple."

"So let's see," concluded Elfman. "A very pleasant non-singing golf master gave thousands of people another good-to-great concert for a kid's charity that I'm still not sure what it does. Ah, another night in Vegas."

But Tiger does love music, just not this music. He's into R&B and hip-hop. And his foundation seems vague to Elfman and others simply because it's the kind of charity that gives money to other charities, like the United Way. Therefore its own identity is a little hazy. They try to explain it on the Web site. "Dear Friends," reads a letter there from Tiger, "when I was younger, my Dad encouraged me to change the world. He taught me that anything is possible . . . through the Tiger Woods Foundation, I'm able to use golf as a vehicle to reach out to children and families. . . . With your help, I believe we can make a difference." Page two, Part III of the foundation's tax return describes its reason for being a little more succinctly: "GOLF CLINICS TO ENCOURAGE YOUNG PEOPLE TO SUCCEED THROUGH EDUCATION, SPORTS, AND HARD WORK AND TO ENCOURAGE YOUNG INNER CITY GOLFERS."

Woods, a man of mixed race from a middle-class background, wants to change the world by helping others with ethnicity or economics in shouting distance of his own. Well-off white children may be as hungry as anyone for inspiration and example, but they are not his target audience. The foundation's beneficiaries tell the story: the Urban Junior Golf Association in Tampa, Florida, received $27,000 from the Tiger Woods Foundation. The Asian Counseling and Referral Services in Seattle got $5,000. The National Minority Junior Golf Foundation Scholarship Foundation got $5,000. The Joy of Sports Foundation in

Alexandria, Virginia, got $1,500. And New York Youth at Risk received $1,800.

That seems like nickels and dimes for an organization that began life in December 1996 with $2.5 million, half a million dollars from Tiger and $2 million donated by corporations. And although the foundation raises a couple of million a year and now claims assets of almost $10 million, in its first five years of existence it had donated only $1.5 million. Why hasn't the foundation at least given away the money it raised when it opened its doors? Why are they sitting on so much cash?

Forgive us our cynicism, but by now we've all heard about the greedy ex-jocks who create a foundation, raise money—often through a golf tournament—employ friends and family, and at the end have such high "administrative expenses" that the charity doesn't get very much. Doug Sanders, for example, was caught with his hand in his own charitable cookie jar a few years ago in Houston, paying himself a couple hundred thousand for not much work. Barry Bonds ran a little charity thing that raised $60,000—but $45,000 of that went to an executive fee—for his mother. Michael Jordan's now-disbanded JUMP Inc. employed his brother, sister, and brother-in-law. The salaries earned by the officers of some of the big national charities are a scandal. The Tiger Woods Foundation tweaks suspicion when it won't give you any more than window dressing when you ask for financial information. Then you learn that in July 2001 *USA Today* published an analysis of athletes' charities—but that the Tiger Woods Foundation did not participate in the survey. Something smells fishy.

But there's no fish. Although the TWF is more conservative than a blue suit, it conducts itself perfectly legally. According to its tax return, on file with the California attorney general's office, the big bank account is not a barrier hiding generous salaries; President Earl Woods and his board of directors don't accept a dime. The foundation's executive director gets paid $85,000 per year, less than half what other $10-million charities pay their head men. The TWF strategy seems to be to let income exceed outgo in order to build an endowment of, say, $25 million to $30 million, at which point generous checks can be written from the interest earned. (And at which point Tiger and Earl's control will be thorough indeed, since donations and donators will be far less important.) Many charities fail because in their zest to give away what they take in, they don't take an early opportunity to be self-sustaining. Keeping the cash at home for a while is a conservative and confident strategy, nothing sinister about it. They know what they're doing at the Tiger Woods Foundation.

Why they act like they're hiding something is another question. Like the boss himself, his charity wants your money and your approval. And it wants you to keep your distance.

SO TIGER'S COOL WITH THE IRS and with the thousands of kids who've seen him hit a golf ball. But how does he get along with the other guys on the Tour? Because just as high school isn't only about Spanish class, the world of big-time golf isn't only concerned with low scores. Locker rooms and buffets and practice greens are shared, and everyone has the same basic job. With home games a rarity for everyone, some golf pros often develop a brotherhood of the road, like long-haul truckers. Of course, this forced familiarity also sometimes breeds contempt. Although professional golf has its share of loners, socialization is part of the life. You've got to bring a support system—a wife, kids, girlfriends, friends, and for a few, an entourage—or find one.

Woods, of course, was a special case. Cameras and bright lights followed him up the steps on his first day at PGA Tour High School. Mighty corporations named Nike and IMG marched alongside. He contended in his second tournament, and won in his fifth. He didn't wait in any lines: On the first day of class, he was Most Likely to Succeed, and within months he was palpably the best student in the whole damn school. Friendships with the incumbents plainly weren't that important to him. He was not Most Popular.

For example, before the first round of the Mercedes Championships in 1997, at the giddy height of Tigermania, Woods and his forty-year-old playing partner David Ogrin did what players always do before teeing off. They shook hands with the dignitaries, introduced themselves to their scorers, counted their clubs, and allowed the Darrel Survey person to examine the make and model of all their equipment. Another part of the first tee ritual requires contestants to disclose to each other the kind of golf ball they'll be using. I've got a Titleist 3, David," Tiger said. "What are you playing?"

"A little white ball," Ogrin said icily—and without looking up, saying almost nothing but speaking volumes.

For another example, on the practice tee at Colonial Country Club in Fort Worth, Davis Love III, the son of a teaching pro, was helping his perfectionist friend Tom Kite tinker with his club position at the top of his backswing. Kite, the U.S. Open champion of 1992 and one of the most successful players ever, works on his game like a coal miner. A small crowd leaned in to watch his high-level lesson with Love. Then Tiger strode through the ropes, and the angels sang, and the entire gallery seemed to gasp. Almost every fan and writer, and every talking head and minicam, scurried to the far end of the tee to watch Woods, the real show. Kite regarded the stampede as he bumped another ball from the pile. "And there goes the greatest player in history," he muttered with heavy sarcasm.

Tiger's weary sangfroid combined with his youth and his success initially rubbed a lot of his fellow competitors on the Tour the wrong way. Guys he defeated in the U.S. Amateur or U.S. Junior surfaced to tell you that Tiger looks through them as if they're made of very clear glass—which isn't really such a slam on Tiger, when you think about it. His ability to see nothing but targets and think of nothing but goals may be why he won and they lost. On the other hand, you hear this from Kaye Kessler, a reputable observer who has never lost to Tiger: "He was a total pain in the ass."

"After Tiger won the NCAA in Memphis," says Kessler, who wrote sports for forty-three years for the *Columbus* (Ohio) *Citizen-Dispatch,* "Jack brought him up here on his plane to receive the College Golfer of the Year award during the last round of the Memorial. This is in May 1996. At the ceremony, Jack's wearing a coat and tie and Tiger's in golf clothes, slouching, just as bored as can be. I thought it was an affront to Jack and to the occasion. He couldn't have been less interested or cooperative, and he wanted to be taken back to the airport almost as soon as he got here."

Fatigue and youth likely worked against Woods back then, and surely a bit of something else—arrogance or shyness, depending on who's telling the story. "I introduced myself at his first pro tournament [fall 1996]," says Mark Calcavecchia. "He was pretty standoffish at first, and he wouldn't sign things for the other guys, for their charities. Then he had that goof-up when he canceled out of his own banquet. But I think he's done an awesome turnaround. I can't think of anyone on the Tour who dislikes him."

Several things have made Tiger a lot more likable to his peers, and first among these may be the realization that his assaults on par were nothing personal. Whatever Tiger was chasing, it was never them. He pursued swing perfection and major championships, not Davis Love III. And despite a temper that is only a little less combustible than that of Steve "Volcano" Pate, and a profound self-centeredness, in time Woods revealed himself to his peers as a pretty good guy and a good sport. They admire and respect his capacity for hard work, and his excellence, and they liked it when Earl receded from the scene. Racial condescension melted in the face of athletic superiority.

Best of all, like Arnold Palmer in 1960, Tiger elevates the sport, which benefits everyone. There's more money and attention for every pro golfer. Reflected glory is still glory.

But circumstance keeps Tiger from being one of the boys. First of all, one-of-the-boyhood is not that big a deal on the Tour. Golf is a social game, but professional golf is not. It attracts independent, withdrawn types, competitive sons of bitches, most of whom approach the forced familiarity of the Wednesday pro-am with dread. Like most of his peers, Woods is disinclined to see a golf tournament as an occasion to make friends. And he handles his time in such a regimented way that you can't help but be reminded that he is the son of a military man. He has his press segment, and his play segment, and lunch, perhaps a bit of business with Agent Steinberg, a workout or two, an autograph interval, and two practice periods. Trouble brews when you request a signature on your hat during lunch or ask him a question during practice, or any combination that doesn't match his plan. Tiger pretends not to hear the inappropriate request, or he'll freeze a miscreant's blood with just a look. And blank-faced men from security are always nearby.

"He never stops," says Brandel Chamblee, one of the smartest and funniest players on Tour, and a potential friend that Tiger will probably never have. "I might say 'Hi, Tiger,' and he'll say, 'Hi Brandel,' but he's got so many people pulling on him, he's got to be a moving target.

"Listen, you can't have the whole package in this era. The top guy can be a great player or he can be funny and friendly. The last guy to accomplish both was Lee Trevino. We could do far worse than Tiger Woods. What if our top player had been John Daly?"

And lest we forget, every minute on the pro Tour is a competition. Who can hit the most balls, lift the most weight, win the most money? Tiger can, that's who, a fact that discourages as many as it inspires. "I don't think you could get any of us to admit we're going through the motions," says Chamblee. "But it's like chasing Secretariat. If we were honest, we'd admit that we're just trying to close the gap a little bit, and increase the number of tournaments we might compete with him from two or three to seven or eight."

Curtis Strange, at forty-six more an astute observer than a championship challenger, sees "some guys who are defeated on the first tee" when paired with Woods. "It's not that they give up, but they really don't expect to beat him, either," Strange says. "They say they'll work harder to catch up, but I don't see how they can try any harder than they already are."

Tiger's slowed down enough to develop relationships with at least four of his contemporaries—Cook, O'Meara, Calcavecchia, and Duval. Why these guys? All are significantly older—John, Mark, and Mark are in their forties, and David, at thirty, is five years Tiger's senior. They're all well met—although Duval's a tough onion to peel—and each has a lively intelligence that at least matches Tiger's. Each of the four has known spectacular success, from juniors to college to the Tour. Like Woods, O'Meara and Cook won the U.S. Amateur; like Woods, O'Meara, Calcavecchia, and Duval won the British Open. On a deep level, you suspect that Tiger believes these four have something to teach him, which is not a bad basis for a friendship.

But Tiger's a teacher, too, especially to his two Isleworth neighbors. "I think he's had an impact on everybody in golf," O'Meara says. "I know he's been a benefit to me personally. His youth, his determination, his desire to be one of the best ever pushed me a little. There's a strong possibility that I might not have won the Masters and the British Open without that." O'Meara was forty-one when he birdied the last two holes to beat Duval at Augusta; later in his wonderful summer of '98 he defeated Brian Watts in a playoff for the Open at Royal Birkdale.

"Except for Mark, I've probably played more golf with him than anyone," says Cook, who has won ten times on the Tour. "I'll tell you, he tests you out there. . . . He's made me step up a few things, in terms of fitness and mental-wise. I watch him on the practice range, and he's not just grabbing a ball and slapping it out there. He's *motivated.*"

Duval says yeah, he and Tiger may have become friends in recent years simply because both are represented by IMG, and both represent Nike. Neither has kids, neither is married—although Duval has had a long-term relationship with a thin, beautiful blonde named Julie MacArthur. Neither is particularly fond of the prying press. Both live in very large houses in Florida and both own games far above all but a handful of golfers now on the planet. They're different, too, of course, especially in what they focus on off the course. Duval has a Thoreau-like wish for simplicity, which is why he dumped all his clothing and equipment endorsements in favor of a soup-to-nuts deal with Nike, giving him more time for good books and snowboarding—

and spurring a lawsuit from Acushnet, his previous club and ball dealer. Tiger, on the other hand, involves himself in all the myriad aspects of his empire, from the pixel arrangement in the Tiger Woods Nintendo game to helping Buick develop a new two-seater called the Bengal to encouraging young inner-city golfers.

David's recently streamlined and muscular body is often cited as evidence of Tiger's influence. But it's hard to tell. Duval says he started to work out and eat better simply because he wanted to get fit, and Tiger's delts and distance off the tee had nothing to do with it. With the calm regard of his unblinking blue eyes, talking with Duval is like talking with Ben Hogan, intimidating, and revealing more in what is not said than in what is said. Every question is carefully weighed, and no answers are given reflexively. For example, you ask him if he feels like he's always chasing Tiger.

Pause. "Sorry, I don't think I can help you on that."

What about your narrow loss to Tiger at the Masters, David. Did it depress you for a time, or perhaps it inspired you to your great victory later in the year?

"No, it didn't inspire me," he says. "And no, I wasn't depressed. I've been there. I played great and I didn't win."

So is resilience your greatest strength, or one of them?

"I don't know. Maybe that's for you to say."

So let's say it: Duval's remorselessness as a competitor is an awesome strength and it exists completely apart from Eldrick. But how each guy affects the other is the most interesting question, one we'll have to figure out for ourselves over time, since neither seems likely to bare his soul.

But one specific impact is clear: Tiger's number one in the world rankings, by a wide but shrinking margin, and David's number three.

The fourth super-friend is a thick open book named Mark John Calcavecchia. The only one of the group to have known much golf adversity, he cruised the United States for four years in the early eighties, driving a three-speed black and silver Camaro into the ground, barely making a living as a golf professional. Everything he owned sprawled on the backseat and in the trunk, covered with a blanket of beer cans, cassette cases, and Big Mac wrappers. For succor in those lonely days and nights of minitours and missed cuts, Calc would find the biggest, noisiest building in town, with cars in its lot like his own. Then he'd rummage beneath his clubs and clothes until he found his "rock"—his bowling ball. Actually, he traveled with two fourteen-pounders, the unmistakable sign of a committed keggler.

Bright lights, small city: the hiss of a rolling rock on maple boards, the resounding crash of the pins, the smells of frying onions, beer, BO, and foot powder—all of it took Calc back to his happy place, Hillside Bowl in Laurel, Nebraska. His dad ran the place, and Mark hung out there. He did exactly what you'd expect: He mastered the pinball machine, unstuck the bowling pins, ran his bowling average up to 185, filled up the paper towel machine in the men's room, and operated the lane conditioner—not that big a job, since Hillside had only eight lanes. A big kid with great hands, Mark played center on the basketball team and full-back on the football team. He was good at any game he tried.

Like bowling, golf was a present from his father. Little Laurel (population one thousand) didn't have a place to play. "So Dad and his buddies bought a cornfield just outside of town and built a golf course," Calc says. "No hills, no irrigation, basically just four hundred yards out and four hundred yards back." The seven-year-old tagged along with his elders, who let him putt. When the father saw that his son could actually hit the ball, he bought him a junior set of Powerbilts.

The family moved to Palm Beach, Florida, when Mark was thirteen. His father had multiple sclerosis and just couldn't take the Great Plains winters anymore. "We got there in July, and I played all through the winter," Calc recalls. "That's when I realized I was decent." More than decent, the big kid from Nebraska with a bad grip could compete with any of the local hotshots his age, including Jack Nicklaus's son Jackie. In February 1974, Mark's older brother Nick took him to his first PGA Tour event, the Jackie Gleason Inverrary Classic. Chimes went off in his head like noon in a clock store: "That's when I knew I wanted to be a pro. Every year after, I went to Inverrary and Doral.

"And I never paid to get in," Calc adds proudly. "You could just park by a condo and walk right in."

"Grinder" is the golf word for a painstaking player, someone who compensates for a lack of talent or technique with an accountant's intolerance for mistakes. Calc is the instinctive opposite: He's a rocker. He plays golf and lives life by feel. So he doesn't mind if his hotel is a half-hour drive from the tournament site, because that gives him time to hear an entire side of Rush or AC/DC on his twenty-four-disc player.

Fame and money disguise it, but the main branch of Tiger's male friends have blue collars beneath their two-hundred-dollar shirts. Instructor Butch Harmon, father Earl, caddie Steve Williams, and Calcavecchia can all tell a joke, use the f word in a wide variety of contexts, and handle themselves in a biker bar. Calc's not hanging with Tiger to learn anything, or to soak up any of the rock star atmosphere. For Tiger, Calc's just a friend, a good guy.

"Nah, Tiger hasn't had any effect on me," Calcavecchia says. *"I'm* trying to influence *him*. But after two beers, he's done. We've gotta work on that."

WHILE TIGER IS AWAY, the lesser carnivores play. You spot the one you've been looking for on the fringe of the practice green at the TPC Woodlands, site of the Shell Houston Open. The most memorable character of Charles Howell's rookie year stands in a tangle of chipping and putting golf pros on an April morning hitting six-yard flop shots. A lot of the other guys are chatting among themselves and with equipment reps and agents but Frank Lickliter is alone in the crowd. Immaculate in dark pants, white shirt, and black and white shoes, he's six-one, two hundred, with wide shoulders that make him seem even bigger. Like Duval, Big Frank hides the window to his soul behind dark, wraparound shades. If books were covers, he'd be the bouncer at a club you probably don't belong in. Or perhaps he's the uniformed man with a radio and a gun walking slowly from his cruiser to your car window. The man who caught you doing seventy in a fifty is thirty-two but looks older.

When you get closer you see the dusting of white stubble on his ruddy face—he didn't shave today. Then you notice a final part of his presentation, common thirty or more years ago but now not much seen—a burning cigarette that stays clamped between his lips when he chips.

For a few minutes you admire the precision and delicacy of his shots, which land just short of the hole then roll two reluctant feet and almost go in. His caddie, a blond stump of a man named Tony, retrieves the four balls and walks them back to the boss's feet for another repetition, and another and another. When the golfer finally pauses to adjust his smoke, you take the opportunity to introduce yourself.

Franklin Ray Lickliter II listens carefully and reacts slowly to the idea of being written about in a book. "Well, yeah, you're right," he says. "I *am* different from these other guys . . . I drive a Hummer." He bought his macho military machine in '99 to celebrate his success in '98, when he won $872,000—all of which he may need for gas. But vehicle choice is only a detail, just a part of a slightly unusual life that produced a slightly unusual man. No rich daddy AJGA childhood for Frank: He grew up without inherited wealth in landlocked Franklin, Ohio, north of Middletown and south of Centerville, in the deep country between Cincinnati and Dayton. His father made forty thousand dollars a year working in the mill for Armco Steel, which is the key to his story. Armco built a great golf course called Shaker Run for its employees and their children, and Frank wore it out.

Because he stayed close to home as a junior golfer, "Frank didn't have a national or even a statewide reputation," says Fred Jefferson, his college coach at Wright State University in Dayton. "But right from the start, he could win any tournament he played in. He was the hardest worker we've ever had." But Frank had a temper. Infuriated by a missed short putt during a college tournament at Windmill Lakes Golf Club, Kent State's home course, Frank took a hefty divot out of the second green. Frank replaced the turf and accepted a two-shot penalty from Herb Page, Kent's red-faced coach. Lickliter must have wanted to succeed very badly.

"He's been good to our program," says Jefferson. "He's donated to our fundraiser and he's come back to speak to the team. And just dropping his name really helps in recruiting."

A *Hummer*, Frank, you say. Jesus. You mention that you've just spent an hour or two with Bob May, another man who loves his motor vehicles, reviewing his razor-thin loss to Tiger at the 2000 PGA. "He got fucked," Frank says, meaning May, referring to a lucky bounce Woods got on the last hole of their playoff. "Tiger's got a golden horseshoe stuck up there somewhere. His ball bounced off a patch of grass this big or it would have been thirty yards deep in the rough."

You mention that the Bob May profile is for *Maximum Golf*. "I love that magazine!" Lickliter says.

He's asked about his schedule. He drags on the weed

and leans on his wedge. "I'm playing Greensboro, New Orleans, and Dallas. Then a break to go hunting. Then Kemper, the Memorial . . ."

What about the hunting, Frank? You know that Lickliter and his friend Fuzzy Zoeller stalked bears in Alaska in spring 2000. What will it be this time? More bears? Birds?

"Prairie dogs," he says. "I've got a friend who's got a 160,000-acre ranch in Wyoming. It's great. Shot fourteen hundred rounds last year."

Tenacious burrowers and prolific breeders, prairie dogs live gregariously in huge "towns." They pop up randomly and bark like Chihuahuas, which makes them sound cute, but *Cynomys ludovicianus* make Swiss cheese out of pasture land. They're a nuisance. Ranchers are happy to get rid of the little bastards.

As Frank describes it, he will fire at the buck-toothed foot-long rodents from a bench on the back of a pickup truck. You try to picture the scene: an umbrella sheltering the bench in the back of the truck; a big Coleman cooler nearby; the wide Wyoming sky; the short sharp crack of the rifle; a rising tide of spent shells filling the bed. Perhaps the hunter hunts in camo with a burning cigarette in his mouth. Perhaps music comes from the cab, perhaps country. Maybe he mutters "gotcha" or "dammit" after each shot. Suddenly this enterprise reminds you of an arcade game called Pop-a-Mole in which plastic mole heads emerge unpredictably from their holes and you score points by whacking them on the head with a rubber mallet before they disappear. You think this comparison is hilarious and you share the thought with Frank, who does not laugh. He indicates that he might talk with you some other time, or he might not. "Call my agent," he says. You're dismissed.

The handful of gallery for Lickliter's threesome on Thursday includes his fiancée, Diane Owen, a thin, regal blonde with perfect posture. Frank's practically perfect, too, at least with the driver, his best club. His stance is wide, his hands are low, and his swing is a beautiful metronome. But he closes the club face a bit at the top of his backswing, which doesn't look so good.

He's having a great year so far but today things just won't fall together. A putt lips out, he gets a buried lie in a bunker, and soon he's a couple over par. He plays the last four or five holes in absolute fury. After unsatisfactory shots, he whacks his golf bag with the grip end of his club, or he drops the club, or throws it at the bag. Caddie Tony picks up the sticks without reacting; he's been in Lickliter's employ for two years, he's used to it. You begin to think the questions you've composed may not be asked, or if asked, not listened to. Frank, your level of emotion is high for out here—what causes it? Has being from a slightly different background from the other guys made you feel like an outsider? Are you down with Tiger's efforts to get poor urban kids into golf? How has Tiger affected you? Did you hunt for the dinner table when you were a kid? Does Diane have a sister?

You've got to try. After the round Frank comes out of the scoring trailer into a little roped-off area reserved for players, caddies, and media. Irate zippers zing open and shut. He's putting glove, ball, and tees into his golf bag the way your woman packs when she's leavin'. He's shot 75. "That's OK, Frank," you say. "You'll shoot 65 tomorrow." He doesn't even slow down as he brushes past.

BACK IN THE DAY when first place was eight hundred dollars, when you joined the Tour you joined a fraternity. Pledges drank and laughed and played cards with the established guys at the end of the day, and no one brought their wives. Only two players dared violate the house rules. Hogan never traveled without Valerie, and he didn't drink with the boys until late in his career. Nelson didn't drink, didn't leave home without Louise, and he didn't hold with gambling.

"Every week we weren't on the lesson tee was a holiday," says Jack Burke, Jr., seventy-three, the 1956 Masters and PGA champ. "We just wanted to stay out there. After three weeks, these guys need a shrink and a chiropractor."

When you're in Houston and you need an antidote to the nonverbal golf pro, you go see Burke, the owner and operator of Champions Golf Club in Houston. He lives to talk and loves a debate: In his era, virtually everyone in his business had a conversational gift. They had to, because their real job was back at Sunny Willows Country Club, selling Mr. Jones a pair of socks and selling his wife on following through on the bunker shot. A really good tee ball went 250, no one knew from endorsements, drivers were flammable, and no one played the Tour full-time. Things have changed.

"They're chasing Tiger—we were always chasing Snead," Burke says. "When he hit that one iron and you felt the ground move, you knew you better go after it with a persimmon. But there was not a lot of oohing and ahhing after I hit.

"No, I wouldn't compare Tiger to Hogan, or to Snead. He's more like Bobby Jones. Creative, developing shots all the time. He didn't get that from Butch [Tiger's instructor Butch Harmon is Burke's close friend]. Neither Butch nor his father [Claude Harmon, the pro at Winged Foot who won the '48 Masters] could do that. At the same time, Tiger's very scientific, and on plane."

Burke's father was the most influential club professional of the last century. A Philadelphian transplanted by oil money to Houston, Jack Burke, Sr., was first in an almost biblical progression of instructors. He taught Jack Grout, who taught Jack Nicklaus; he taught Jimmy Demaret, who won the Masters three times; and he taught Harvey Penick. Harvey sat at the master's knee with a red notebook, which much later became the hugely successful Little Red Book. Harvey taught Tom Kite and Ben Crenshaw, and through his books, thousands more. Burke Junior's reputation and knowledge are such that Hal Sutton comes to him for swing lessons and Phil Mickelson shows up asking for help with his putter. Burke has a full head of gray hair and the great eyes of a leading man. When he interviewed for club pro jobs as a much younger man, he'd go ahead and put the unspoken but obvious issue on the table: I'm not after your wife or your daughter, he'd say, now or ever. The interviewer would sigh with relief and offer him the job.

"Why is Tiger so good? Let's start at the beginning," says Burke, leaning forward in his leather CEO chair. Except for the door hole, each of his four office walls are lined with books. No windows; it's in the center of the Champions clubhouse. "Tiger's got the time, the hours to put in. He's got no wife or kids. These other guys are giving the wife a break by taking the kids to the mall.

"Second: He hits it so far and he's one of the best putters who ever lived. He's got the touch of [the infamous safe cracker] Willie Sutton. He *likes* putting—these other guys act like they're *enduring* it. He's a creative person, which you must be to be a great reader of greens, and he's brave enough to putt what he reads.

"Then there's this word—trust—a theological term. In golf, it's trusting your swing, your hands, and your timing for five hours. Trust is letting go, like a father letting go of his kid on a swing. He's trusting the rope. Trust comes from playing the game *as a game*. These other guys are not playing golf, they're playing celebrity. Where they are versus where they think they are, well, I'd like to buy some of that real estate. But Tiger—I haven't seen anyone enjoy golf as much. Chi Chi had that ability and so did Trevino, Palmer, Snead, Hogan. Hogan had a playful side. He didn't show it on his face, but he was adjusting for that game twenty-four hours a day. Sugar Ray Robinson just loved to fight, loved the chance to throw the perfect left hook. At age eighty-five, Vladimir Horowitz was practicing eight hours a day."

We look at Woods and see a modern superstar with a jet and a financial empire. Burke sees a throwback, and the quaintest athletic cliché, a man who plays for the love of the game.

None of them mind getting paid for it, but Woods's two closest competitors also love golf for golf's sake. Duval, of course, doesn't show it, because like Hogan he doesn't show anything. Burke hasn't worked with him, but you sense he'd like to. First he'd change his grip—which is very strong—to a more neutral hold. "He'd feel his shots better," Burke says. Then he'd remove Duval's trademark wraparound Oakleys, which would "make him less like a robot marching down the fairway. These guys in their sunglasses look like astronauts on a mission to the moon."

Mickelson he knows far better. With his modest smile and his altar-boy looks, we all feel we know Phil. He is a generous man. When he heard that a writer's young daughter was mortally ill with a brain tumor, he asked the writer to tell him all about it. The color drained from Phil's face as he listened, then he offered to write a check for twenty thousand dollars to help with the medical expense. But there's a fascinating and dark river flowing beneath Mickelson's calm surface. He's addicted to the high-risk shot—in business, in Vegas, and on the golf course. He's a gambler, sometimes a very good one, on football and baseball and at baccarat. But the iron rule of gambling is that the house usually wins. Why else would the casinos be so nice and big? "Phil's a great kid, but he does have this tendency to go for things more than he should," says Burke.

A case in point occurred in February, on the seventeenth hole at the Buick Invitational at Torrey Pines in San Diego. It was the third hole of a playoff, and Phil, who had won seventeen times on the Tour, had the honor against a nervous opponent. With Purgatory right and trees left, the situation seemed to beg for a lay-up. Mickelson hit driver—dead right into the canyon. Frank Lickliter, showing the brain-draining emotion of a man who has never won on the Tour, also hit driver, and also hit it in the big hole. They both hit provisionals and made the fairway. But both original tee shots were found, so for a third time they had to return to the tee. And there was Phil, still saying screw you to safety. He whaled away with the driver, and his ball flew on a familiar vector toward the canyon. But he got lucky, as gamblers sometimes do. His ball hit a tree. He chopped it on from there and two-putted for a 6. Lickliter hit two very good shots and had a six-foot putt for the glory and $630,000. He three-putted. Mickelson had won with a double bogey, and no one could remember the last time that happened.

In addition to his allergy to playing safe, one other thing may keep Phil a mere moon orbiting planet Tiger: He has never won one of golf's majors. Whether these four tournaments are really so vital to his curriculum vitae is debatable, but Mickelson believes so, and is in fact obsessed with the idea. "He feels that Jesus put him down here to win a major," says Burke. "But God did not put you on earth to prevail in a game."

Finally, you say thanks, see you in the fall, because Burke and Champions are hosting the last big tournament of the year, the Tour Championship. By the way, you ask by the door, what should these guys do to catch up? Tiger seems so far ahead. "Unless they make some changes, they'll never do it. And that's hard, because they all take lessons from the same guys. Anyway, for their own good, they better not be chasing Tiger. They better be chasing themselves."

CHARLES HOWELL III comes to Houston chasing a number. He's got to win about one hundred thousand dollars to play the Tour for the rest of the year, and he has six more tournaments in which to do it.

But if his life feels like a fraying rope or a ticking clock, he's awfully good at hiding it. Off the course, Howell is relaxed and cheerful. On it, his game is sincere and businesslike, with no look of desperation, and no crazy shots attempted. For the most part he hits to the center of the green and two-putts. A couple of times he misses greens and fails to make par. The result is a first-round 73, the cautious and slightly rusty first-round of a guy in only his third Tour event of the year.

Yet twenty or so aficiandos walk with him every step, and after he hits they whistle and whisper "*damn.*" For never have they seen a golf ball driven like this, or a golf swing so close to the modern ideal. Like Woods, Howell combines the wiry strength of a rodeo cowboy with the best fundamentals money and practice can buy. Tiger is more exciting, because he can get wild and hit it two fairways over. He loses his balance sometimes and has to catch himself with a little half step, and occasionally he follows through with the club in such a wacky place that you know he's trying awfully hard. But Howell always keeps his feet under him and he plays more standard shots with his standard swing than does Tiger, and his regular shot is such a bullet you can hardly credit it.

Howell seldom lines up in the modern way, from behind the ball. With driver in hand, he puts the ball on a tee as high as a toilet paper roll, and says "left center?" to Bambi, his caddie. "Yep, left center," Ron "Bambi" Levin replies pleasantly. "It's 330 to the far side of the bend. Take it right at that tree." Howell takes a couple of slow-motion practice backswings and makes his right hand pass his left on the way down, something that neither he nor anyone else would do intentionally when they actually hit the ball. Then, his other quirk, just before he unleashes the thunder: He holds up his right hand and wiggles it, to get a cheap-looking metal bracelet to slip down over the bump of the ulna bone on his wrist.

In some ways, Howell is to Woods as Jack was to Arnie. Charles, at age twenty, is Nicklaus, the calm, purposeful technician. Tiger, twenty-five, is emotional and resourceful, and charisma radiates from him like rays from the sun. Howell, no fist-pumper, reacts to even spectacular shots as if he expected them to happen.

They go back a long way, as competitors, not as friends. Twice they intersected at big amateur events in Portland, Oregon. Unprecedentedly large crowds flocked to the 1993 U.S. Junior at Waverly Country Club to see Woods, the two-time defending champion. But a large part of the gallery became enamored of the little kid from Georgia. Howell was fourteen then, five foot five and ninety-five pounds, and the lenses on his glasses seemed too big for his face. He carried four woods in his bag—driver, two, five, and seven, but he won match after match against bigger, older kids. Finally, he lost in the semifinals. Tiger, then seventeen, defeated Ted Oh in the other semi and went on to win his third straight Junior. Which Earl, incidentally, believes to be his son's greatest feat.

Three years later, a similar scenario played out at Pumpkin Ridge. Thousands of Portlanders turned out to see if Tiger could win his third consecutive U.S. Amateur, just as he'd won three Juniors. But he faced a formidable test in the third round—Howell. Bob Robinson of the *Portland Oregonian* referred to him as "the slight opponent with the high-powered swing." Robinson spoke to one Ditsy Zener during their match. "It's really tough not to root for Howell, but I'm a Tiger fan," said Ditsy. "He's such a good role model. I'm sure the other boy is too, but I don't know that much about him." Tiger won, three-and-one.

Howell talks for a while after his first round at Houston about the few things that have surprised him about the golf tourist's life. Giving or getting autographs is not new to him—he used to ask for them himself when he was a kid, by the eighteenth green at Augusta National, and he signed a few himself even before he turned pro. And he was aware of the existence of an autograph industry with adults as its foot soldiers, but he's been startled by the rude insistence of the autograph seekers. "It's out of hand," Howell says. "If you don't sign, or you don't sign enough, they say you're a jerk. The whole thing's demeaning to both parties. I don't see any real value in it."

Other rookies have been felled by the grind of the

never-ending road and the level of competition on the Tour, but neither has surprised him, Howell says. However, an emotion he'd rarely felt on a golf course washed over him the last time he played—fear. He'd hit the green in 2 on the par 5 final hole at Atlanta, and faced an eagle putt that was like thirty feet of frozen pavement, downhill. Two putts were all he wanted, or needed, but taking three putts might be devastating in several ways. Caddie Ron "Bambi" Levin chose his words carefully: "Bet you can't leave it short." Howell exhaled loudly. "I'm shakin' so bad I might hit it in the water," he whispered. But he caressed his Callaway Red to three feet and wiggled the next one in. He tied for sixth and won $103,290, his first check of the year.

The money must be a comfort, but does he feel alone out there? Well, no—he's got Heather for company most weeks. She finishes her education classes at Oklahoma State on Thursday, then gets on a plane to wherever Charles is. (Apropos of his dislike of being alone and his distaste for the petty details of travel, she's lately begun to call her man the Princess.) But can a newcomer—especially a threateningly good one—enter such a dog-eat-dog world and make friends? Yes, the Thin Man says, he likes most of the guys. Gary Nicklaus and his girlfriend, for example, have become particularly good pals to Charles and Heather. "But Brett Ogle told me the difference between our tour and the European Tour: at breakfast, they have one table and seven guys. We have seven guys and seven tables."

One other thing: He hadn't understood how desperately the manufacturers want you to play their equipment:

"TaylorMade will pay anyone in the field $3,500 to tee it up on Thursday with their driver. Titleist pays $750 if you use their putter. Similar deals for golf balls and putters. Some guys take the money then switch after Thursday; they don't check after that."

He looks out the dining-room window at the swirl of golf pros and spectators and cars and golf carts. "Golf's a funny game," he says. "No, it's a stupid game. I've stayed up a lot of nights trying to figure it out and I've decided that the less you think about it, the better."

Howell shoots another 73 the next day. You watch him give an interview afterward, in the media corral next to the scoring trailer. He's a natural at this, saying things he didn't just think of but not sounding the least bit rehearsed. "I'm the oldest of a generation who looked up to Tiger," he says. "We looked up to him and to his accomplishments. He's defined how the game should be played today." Yes, he says, the travel's tough, you really have to pace yourself. What about your goals, asks Jimmy Burch of the *Fort Worth Star-Telegram*. He's *really* ready for this one: "First, to get my conditional status so that I can play the Tour for this year," Howell says. "Second, to get my card for next year. And third, to get in the top fifty in the World Rankings, because the top fifty get invited to the Masters."

But he makes no progress in Houston—his 146 misses the thirty-six-hole cut. Down now to five tournaments in which to win one hundred thousand dollars, Howell retreats to his and Heather's apartment in Edmond, north of Oklahoma City. He takes a week to practice and reflect on this big numbers game, and then he heads to New Orleans.

APRIL GIVES WAY TO MAY and Tiger reappears, to stand with Byron Nelson under a river birch tree. Tiger towers like an oak at this moment in golf and in life, and respect bordering on awe follows him everywhere. For not only is he the first simultaneous holder of the four modern majors *ever,* he's also graceful in word and deed, and rich, young, and handsome. He's got the best celebrity smile since Jack Nicholson, and the best golf game since Watson, or perhaps Trevino. Modesty whispers that you shouldn't stare when he's just getting a drink of water in Irving or taking a banana from a cooler in Columbus but it's impossible to take your eyes off him. You think you're a sophisticate but still you gape like a rube on the midway.

At the Nelson, a writer sits in the airy press room, which will again be two indoor tennis courts next week. Though he feels like he's hitting on a girl out of his league, he scratches out a letter to Tiger, the most popular kid in school. He puts the note inside the top book of three rubber-banded together and takes the package to the locker-room attendant, who promises to deliver it to the correct cubicle.

Dear Tiger,

While I know you get scores of requests for one-on-one interviews every day, I hope you will consider this one. I'm writing a book called Chasing Tiger *about your effect on everyone and everything in golf. You're making history, and I'm trying to write it, so I hope you'll give me ten minutes this week—or soon—and ten minutes at the end of the year. If you have any interest in this, please call me at . . .*

I hope you enjoy the books.

Sincerely . . .

But there is no response.

May means the Memorial, Jack's tournament, and Tiger always plays, and for the last two years, he's won. But any hope you have of an unscheduled thirty seconds is quickly dashed at the most media-unfriendly event on the PGA Tour. The press is the enemy in Dublin, Ohio. No, you can't go in the locker room. No sir, I'm sorry, the clubhouse is off-limits. You walk out onto the practice tee and three guys in green jackets intercept you like they've been waiting to do this for a year, which they have. No, they say. No, no, no. Jack's event and the Masters are the only events on the Tour that do not allow any informal contact between the princes and the paupers with pens.

But resourceful writers learn to go around roadblocks. Guy Yocom, the *Golf Digest* editor who has cowritten Tiger's new instruction book and is dying to know what Woods thinks of the draft pages, or if he's read them at all, executes a move so clever it should be taught in journalism schools. Yocom knows that on Wednesday afternoon, the earnest volunteers in gray-green sport coats cannot keep track of everyone on the practice tee, for that is the day of the annual Memorial Golf Clinic, a demonstration by a handful of notables in the field. Defending champion Woods will hit, as will Howell. Nicklaus commentates—"Now show us the shot you'll hit on sixteen," he says, or, "Can you hit a high fade with that club?" The Golf Channel televises, and a grandstandful watches. Introducing Howell, with whom he'd played a practice round the day before, Nicklaus says, "When people ask me who among the young fellas can challenge Tiger, I tell them this young man, Charles Howell III."

Yocom, in sunglasses and prematurely gray hair, watches Tiger warm up from fifty feet away, so near and yet so far. A cartoon light bulb illuminates above his head, and he reaches into his pocket for his cell phone and pushes a button. "Butch!" he says. "Yeah, Guy Yocom. Great, yourself? . . . On the practice tee at Memorial, nice day, a little cloudy. . . . Yeah, I'm watching him hit right now. You want to talk to him? Sure, just a minute."

Holding the cell phone aloft like an altar boy with a cross, Yocom walks boldly toward the Man. The well-dressed security force converges on him like gray-and-green F-16s. "It's for Tiger!" Yocom says sternly, and keeps walking. "It's Butch Harmon for Tiger!" Woods notices the commotion. He stops hitting, turns, and accepts the phone from his collaborator. As Tiger talks, the green jackets withdraw, and Yocom remains. After a brief chat with his instructor, Woods returns the phone and resumes hitting wedges. After the second one, he turns to Yocom. From fifty feet, it's easy to read his lips: "Hey, Guy," Tiger says with a little smile. "That was pretty fuckin' good."

The Memorial yields other treats almost as enjoyable, but a couple of aspects of the would-be fifth major are strangely disappointing. It rains—as it always does for this event—but the responsible parties act like they're surprised, and the hilltop walkways behind the eighteenth green become slick with mud. A handful of red-faced young men, seated behind glass in a ground-level luxury box, hoot and holler and pound the window when someone in their view slips and falls. If the slipper is carrying items from the concession stand, the louts are especially pleased. Just as offensive are the speakers from the dais at the big ceremony by the eighteenth green on Wednesday. As they memorialize this year's Memorial honoree, the late Payne Stewart, they quote the Bible so frequently and sermonize so relentlessly that you want to shout "ACLU! Code Red!" Among those being pounded over the head, sitting politely listening with the other golfers, is the best golfer. Tiger, who grew up with Buddhas in his home, not crosses.

But in Calcavecchia's gallery on Thursday you find someone who knows that the golf course is no place for force-fed piety. "How about a beer?" asks Nick Calcavecchia. "You want a beer? Yeah, let's have a beer." Mark's older brother is "in computers" down in Cincinnati. "I ask him how many tickets he needs," Mark says after his round. "He says 'I only need sixteen.'" Nick's a burly guy with a dark mustache and shorts that show his offensive-lineman legs. "I taught Mark everything he forgot," he says during a nine-hole, two-beer stroll.

More salt of the earth sits in carts or leans against walls outside the bag storage room, until such time as their employers appear. Golf is a waiting game, and no one waits more than caddies.

"How long you been workin' for Andrew?"

"Six, seven weeks."

"You doin' any good?"

"Nah. Made two cuts."

"And I said, 'No way, that'd be my eighth week in a row. I wouldn't be any good to you.' "

"Where you stayin'?"

"Ramada."

"How come I ain't seen you?"

"In '91 here, I'm walking backward down near the ninth green, screwin' around, jabbing Billy Andrade with a putter," says Jeff Burrell, Strange's caddie. "And I miss the bridge." Hilarity ensued as Burrell tumbled into the dark water: "I'm in there with all the goddamn carp. It was hot that day, must have been eighty-five, and my jeans just *stunk*, and they must have weighed two hundred pounds. Next day, there's a little sign there—'Burrell's Bridge.' Jack wasn't too happy about that."

With his cigarette, his attitude, and the stubble on his chin, Burrell's the caddie from Central Casting. Charlie Howell is not, of course, but he's here and in a mood to talk. "We're at Hartford last year, Charles's first event as a pro, so I'm gonna caddie," the surgeon says. "It's raining, and I'm trying so hard to keep the clubs dry. I give him a yardage in the first fairway and he just airmails the green, easily twenty yards over. Charles says, 'Let me see that [yardage] book.' We'd teed off on ten but I gave him the yardage for one. Oh. Sorry."

Dr. Howell can smile. Two weeks before, he couldn't. After the Shell Houston Open, when things looked so grim for his son, Charles made the cut at the Compaq Classic of New Orleans, then shot 63-69 on the weekend. The enormity of the stakes he was playing for—employment for the rest of the year—seemed to make him play better, not worse. On the eighteenth hole he hit his best shot of the year, a full-blooded five iron from a fairway bunker onto the green of statistically the twelfth-toughest hole on the Tour. He finished seventh and won $134,000, great progress, but still short of what he needed to achieve Special Temporary Membership on the PGA Tour.

Rich but insecure, Howell drove through at a McDonald's on the way to the airport and a flight to Dallas for the Verizon Byron Nelson. Numbers: He had his usual, number ten, the chicken sandwich, no fries, and a medium root beer. "That'll be $3.91; please drive to the second window," said the disembodied voice of a south Louisiana teenager. Howell pulled out his cell, and dialed his agent at Hambric Sports Management, Pat Malone. More numbers. Four, the number of sponsor's invitations he had left. Nine thousand, the approximate number of dollars he still needed to win. Three hundred and fifty, the amount the Four Seasons wanted per night, versus eighty-five, the nightly rate at the Hampton Inn. "You can afford the Four Seasons," Malone said. "It's right on the grounds. No travel." The Thin Man hesitated. Malone promised to try to get a better price on the luxury hotel.

Malone succeeded—he talked the reservationist down to $205—but Howell didn't. His 73-68 missed the cut.

Three chances left. But a second-round 65 at Kemper the next week led to a tie for fourteenth and a check for $65,000. His probation over, he and Heather celebrate by ignoring the clubs for a day in favor of the Columbus Zoo. He'd become just the third man ever to play his way onto the Tour this way. Justin Leonard and Tiger Woods were the other two.

Back at the Memorial, the interview room, Wednesday.

> Q: The Tour is looking for someone to rival Tiger Woods. Do you think you could be that guy?
>
> CHARLES HOWELL: Sure. I think one day. Right now, no. Today, probably not. Of course, I don't think anyone's giving him too much trouble right now . . . [but] one day I'd most definitely love to challenge Tiger Woods, that's for sure. . . . My goal is to be the best in the world.

He can do it, he knows he can, and even Jack Nicklaus agrees. Howell plays well again in Columbus, winning another sixty-something. But he recedes from view during the week, because at the Memorial you can't take your eyes off Nicklaus and Woods, who at this moment are like Eisenhower and Kennedy on Inauguration Day, January 1961.

The outgoing president walks up the hill to the eighteenth green. Hip and back problems have put a little stumble in his stride. He's not going to make the cut. Time has shortened his backswing and weakened his eyesight, so he can't hit it as far or putt it as well as he used to. In age, Ike's face reverted to babyhood; not so Nicklaus's; decades in the sun have reddened and roughened his countenance. He's in pretty good shape, with a lot more hair than his father had at the same age and without his jowls. But he looks old.

Applause and whooping from his hometown crowd increase as he walks past the two tall trees and the long fairway bunker and up the hill into the amphitheater. Jack holds his right hand aloft in the gesture of a Hollywood Indian saying "how" while nodding his head in sets of two or three and smiling modestly. What is he thinking? That his putt breaks left to right, and it's quick as the devil? That that trashcan back by the tee needs to be emptied? That this year or next might be his last in his own tournament?

Tiger's thoughts are much easier to read. He has scorched his drive on the seventh hole; by hugging the left side of the wet fairway, just three steps from a bunker, he's reduced his route to the green on the 563-yard par 5. The seventh is a birdie hole that Tiger wants to make an eagle hole, but the air is as cool and dank as a cellar and sandpits and succulent rough guard the smallish green. His fellow competitors acknowledge the conditions by playing their second shots a safe eighty yards short. But Tiger ain't laying up.

He and Williams do not look at each other during their ritual conversation: How far to the front edge? 251. How far to the flag? 251 plus 11, 262. What's the wind doing? Stevie pinches off the tops of a few blades and pitches them above his head. A little right to left and against, he says, his voice deep, his accent New Zealand. While still staring at the hole, Woods removes the brown plush toy facsimile of a kiwi that covers his three wood. Like our new president forty years ago, Woods seems both playful and focused on goals higher than the rest of us can perceive.

He's got a style as vivid as JFK's, too. The swinging shaft looks like the spokes of a bicycle wheel, a bicycle going very fast. For most shots, he hits and holds his finish, but when he really swings hard, as now, he whips the club head back almost to the starting line. His shot in the air looks like any other three wood you might see on the practice tee, except it's a bit straighter and a bit longer, and this isn't practice. A couple of minutes later he just misses his eighteen-foot eagle putt, but birdie was never in doubt.

Spurred by a similar shot on the par 5 fifth hole on Sunday—this time a towering two-iron second shot from 249 yards to within a step of the hole—Tiger shoots 68-69-68-66 and wins in a walk. It's his third consecutive win in this event, and his fifth victory in his last six tournaments—it would have been six for six, but all the slumping Tiger could manage at the Nelson was a 63 in the last round and a tie for third. "Tiger is probably the most dominant athlete in the history of sports," says Paul Azinger after Woods's seven-shot win. Azinger often overstates, but Jack Nicklaus doesn't. "I've never seen anybody that's dominated anything more," he says.

And now, the camp followers start to wonder aloud, what about the U.S. Open? Could he successfully defend next month, for his *fifth* major in a row? What an ass kicking that would be! These other guys will have to give up.

* * *

THE NICKLAUS COMPANIES and the Jack Nicklaus Museum Cordially Invite You to a Cocktail Reception and Preview of the Nicklaus Museum. Wednesday, May 30 6:30 p.m to 8:00 p.m.

To get there you go south on the interstate from Muirfield Village, a familiar route for Dubliners who follow Ohio State athletics: The museum sits just off Lane Road, on the western edge of the campus. The Buckeyes' year-old basketball venue—formally the Schottenstein Center at Value City Arena, known by all simply as the Schott—is just across the street. That's the new baseball stadium over there. They were going to build Jack's memorial up by the Memorial, but the neighbors feared traffic and parking problems, and said Not in My Backyard.

The event is lightly attended, a shame because the wine and the hors d'oeuvres and the displays are all superb. Subtle lighting enhances the wholesome fantasy in the carpeted rooms filled with clubs and scorecards and photographs. Each of the major championships has its own space; the mural on the wall makes the Masters room particularly affecting. The dozen or so writers look at the glass cases and listen attentively to the tour guide while struggling with the eternal question of how to eat a plateful of stuffed mushrooms while holding a glass of Chardonnay.

Perhaps you go back to the bar for another glass, and then another, and then go back through the place on your own. What if? you think. What if we put in animatronic robots like the ones in the Hall of Presidents at Disneyland? Press a button and the robots would stand up and not just talk but respond to one question, and they'd be programmed to tell the truth.

Arnie, what do you really think about Tiger?

A living-room setting, with a crackling fire. The ears stand up on the head of the mechanical Golden Retriever at Mr. Palmer's stockinged feet. He swirls the ice in a glass. It all looks real.

"He's as talented as any golfer I've ever seen, and that includes Nicklaus, and Gary Player, and Hogan. He could be the most exciting player in history. Of course, he's had a lot of advantages. So many advantages that I think he's basically had it easy. Did you know I didn't rent a hotel room my first year-and-a-half on the tour? Do you know why? Because I was pulling a goddamn trailer behind my 1953 Impala, that's why. I slept in that. When I won my first tournament, the 1955 Canadian Open, you know what I did with the first-place check? I bought a bigger trailer. We had to count every cent. But Tiger had the coaches and the trainers and the money, a lot of money, the day he turned pro. I was disappointed with how he handled himself early on. Being the best or among the best in this game entails a lot of responsibility and he didn't figure that out for a while. McCormack should have told him. His father should have told him. Tiger's gracious now, which I'm certainly glad to see. But he could be more gracious."

Frank Lickliter, what's the deal?

Big Frank sits behind the wheel of a low, wide Hummer and close to a tall, narrow blonde. Wraparound shades hide what might be his eyes and a Mizuno hat covers the printed circuits on top of his head. He takes a cigarette from his mouth and blows smoke at a NO SMOKING sign.

"Why am I here? Because I won the last tournament before the Memorial. Did any of you assholes in the media even notice? Well, my agent noticed, I'll tell you that. His phone's ringin' off the hook. People with money are calling. So you want me to help you with your book and you're offering what? Nothing? Then that's what you'll get. My time's not free—is yours? Money is the key, not PR, not winning majors. You romantic pussies in the media cannot understand. A major is like an Emmy or an Oscar. An honor. I want to win and I want to get paid, and I'd love to win the U.S. Open. But I'm pretty suspicious of anyone who thinks trophies are so freaking important."

His companion whispers something in his ear. "OK, sorry," Frank says. "I'm a little insecure. I have a temper. A lot of the guys don't like me, as if I give a shit. They call me 'Blade' behind my back because I pulled a hunting knife on this jerk in a bar in Georgia a couple of years ago. TV doesn't like me because I wouldn't go up in the booth to do their stupid interview. But I've got friends, people who like me because I'm honest. Phil Mickelson congratulated me last week, and Ben Crenshaw. Those guys are gentlemen. A lot of these other guys—the hell with 'em."

You walk to the next robot, a meditative, almost inert figure reclining in a fully extended white leather La-Z-Boy. The mechanical man listens to "Blue" by Miles Davis and blows blue cigarette smoke at the dim ceiling light. There's a martini on a table by his right hand.

"Oh, hello. Excuse me if I don't get up," Earl Woods

says. "Have you ever heard anything more real than the sounds from Miles Davis's horn? Let me turn this down. . . . Do I wish to retract my statement comparing my son to Mohandas Gandhi? No, I do not. Or the recent one in which I said Nelson Mandela was one of the few people on this earth who could be considered Tiger's equal? No, I chose my words carefully and I stand by what I said. *Of course* I realize that Mandela was imprisoned for twenty-seven years because he opposed apartheid, and that Gandhi suffered like Jesus on the cross at the hands of the British imperialists in India. Tiger will be a world figure of that stature.

"But you asked what I might like to reconsider. Listening to this music here I . . . well. A lot of it's been luck. My coaching, the psychologists I hired, putting a golf club in his crib—mostly bullshit. Tiger would have been great with me or without me. It's been luck. Luck and weight lifting."

Jack.

You push a chrome button. They're always comparing Tiger to you or you to Tiger. How does that make you feel?

Tropical plants, rattan furniture and a warm breeze give you to understand that this is the Nicklaus home in Florida. As the display comes to life, we see that the animatronic Nicklaus is wearing half-glasses and doing three things at once: watching the Ohio State football team beat Michigan on a big digital TV, jotting notes on a legal pad, and eating shrimp cocktail.

"They can compare Tiger to me all they want," he says, taking off his specs. They've got his blue eyes just right. "Doesn't work. Because it's a different game, as different as football and touch football. Tell you what I mean. Saint Andrews last year. I won two British Opens at Saint Andrews and I promise you every bunker was in play when I played. I was the strongest player in golf and the golf ball did *not* go beyond those bunkers. You couldn't hit it beyond those bunkers. Anybody. And I promise you Tiger wouldn't hit it beyond those bunkers if he was playing the same equipment we were playing. Last summer, he's driving par 4s. Different game.

"Mostly, it's the golf ball. But it's golf clubs, too. I used to feel like if I got it in the fairway with a driver two or three days out of four I had a good chance to win the golf tournament. Now, with the equipment today, I make so many bad swings and I look up and the ball goes straight. You're sitting there, you know, and you say, 'How did that happen?' Now, if you don't hit ten or eleven out of fourteen fairways, you've had a pretty bad driving day. We used to think that was a pretty good driving day.

"Tell you how else it's a different game. When I needed advice, I'd ask my wife. If I needed a lesson, I'd go see Jack Grout. I'd see him; he never went to tournaments with me. But the guys today have a teacher beside them all the time. And a trainer. And a psychologist. That's an expensive thing to have all those guys sitting around on your payroll. We weren't that wealthy. And before they come here, to the Memorial, they call and ask about our child-care facilities. Unbelievable. We're a golf course and a golf tournament, for God's sake. Can you imagine one of us, Arnold or Gary or me, calling Cliff Roberts and saying, 'Can you take care of our kids while we play in the Masters?'

"And you know, fitness-wise, good gracious, we never—lifting weights? You got to be kidding. Exercise? No. Come on, you don't do that, not a golfer. Everybody thought playing tennis was terrible for you, swimming was terrible for you. I played tennis all my life and swam all my life. I think I played in a local basketball league up until I was almost forty. The guys on my team, all younger than me, were great. They'd say to the other team, 'If you take Jack out under the basket, we're taking you out afterward.' Protecting me.

The robot pauses. "But you asked about comparisons. Maybe my approach was different from a lot of fellas today. They say I looked businesslike on the golf course but it was never a business. It was a game. I did what I could to win a game. Played it as a game. Not as a day at the office.

"Now, you know that in the old days of the Tour, everyone was part-time. The real job was at a club somewhere, giving lessons and so on. That ended in the sixties and seventies but we still didn't play golf for a living. We played golf so we could *make* a living. Big difference. Here's what I mean. There wasn't so much in prize money that you could consider yourself wealthy, even in your best year. So we did something else. Arnold had Cadillac dealerships. I had Pontiac dealerships. We both have our own golf course architecture business. We put up our own money. Golden Bear has secretaries, architects, draftsmen, a receptionist, overhead. Endorsements? You think of Tiger, you think of Nike and Buick and Wheaties and American Express, whatever. You get Tiger, you get Nike. But when you think of Jack Nicklaus, you think of . . . what? I'm not identified with any one thing. The money was not there. Compared to today.

"Now there's so much in prize money. . . . We pay $738,000 for first at the Memorial. Players don't need a club job, or a side business. Endorsements are there if they want them but they don't *need* them.

"I'm someone who makes lists and has goals and I decided I'd win as many majors as I possibly could. Tiger's the same way and I wish him luck. But do I want him to break my record? Are you kidding? No. Heck, no."

Tiger! Tiger?

On a table in the foreground sits a tall stack of video games. The Woods robot is putting golf balls on a carpet in a hotel suite, thoroughly absorbed in trying to get his ball to stop inside a circle he's drawn in red Sharpie on a sheet of eight-and-a-half-by-eleven paper. On stage right sits Jerry Chang, part of his Stanford posse. We see the blond, spiked hair on the back of Chang's head, a head that jerks this way and that as he thumbs a little rectangle of plastic, like his hands are riding a surfboard. He's playing Nintendo, the EA Sports Tiger Woods PGA Tour Golf video game for Play Station Two.

Jerry?

"I don't talk to the media," says Chang without turning around. "I don't talk about Tiger with anyone. I respect his privacy, man."

"Oh. Hi," Tiger says. "Sorry. God, I love it here. Lots of visibility, no access. Jack's done a super job. And the food, whoa. The golf course is a lot like Augusta National. Room to drive it, lots of trouble around the greens, no media getting in your face, good crowd control. The greens are perfect. I play pretty good here. Jack inspires me. It's like, you sell insurance or something, right? Well, imagine competing in the Third Quarter Whole Life Contest with the greatest insurance salesman ever. And maybe beating him.

"Listen, you're only allowed one question and technically you've already asked two. So I'll answer the question most people ask: What's it like being me? Well, it's great and it sucks. A contradiction every day. In another culture, in another age, things would be much more pleasant for me. People would be more respectful. The media . . . why do we give any respect to an entire group of people who never do anything, never accomplish anything, but pass judgment on everything? They think they know me. They don't know me.

"There was this eighteenth-century philosopher named Immanuel Kant I read about in a magazine who asked himself, 'What can human beings know with reasonable certainty?' And he concluded: not much. If you can't feel something, taste it, touch it, you can't really know it. You're guessing. So I don't think you're equipped to understand me.

"And I'm not programmed to explain."

4

KEISER, FLECK, OR FIORI

> W—Woods—has a fame that's gone global.
> He has more titles than both Barnes and Noble.
>
> —from "Baby's First Sports Book" by Steve Rushin, *Sports Illustrated*, August 27, 2001

> The most competitive games draw the most competitive men.
>
> —Vince Lombardi

In homage to the inspiration for its very existence, *Maximum Golf* puts Woods on its April cover, a striking, mechanically blurred black and red image of Tiger in extremis, his lips curled, his right hand balled in a celebratory fist. Things seem to be going as well for the magazine as they are for Tiger. Despite an industrywide slump in advertising, *Maximum Golf*'s ad pages are steady, even increasing slightly. They seem to be getting some traction in part because of two important and possibly related discoveries. First, research reveals that *Maximum Golf*'s typical reader is not Tiger's age, as they'd guessed, but ten to twenty years older—still much younger than *Golf Magazine*'s and *Golf Digest*'s typical, mythical reader, a sixty-year-old white man with a slice and a 401(k). And second, they discover that the advertisers hate the cart girl. Ads pay the bills at magazines, not subscriptions, so publisher Mike Caruso and editor Joe Bargmann reluctantly nix the drink chicks pix.

For Tiger's next major victory, at the U.S. Open at Southern Hills in Tulsa, senior editor David Chmeil commissions two photographers and a writer to prepare a preview story. Since the Open rarely leaves a handful of old-money venues in the Northeast—except for occasional stops at Pebble Beach in California—Chmiel wants to know how Oklahoma will be different. In keeping with the magazine's edgy style, the Brooklyn-based photographers Chmeil hires have never shot golf, or sports, except for a little pro wrestling. Their main gig is *Glamour* magazine's fashion Do's and Don'ts. The Don'ts in this popular pictorial—such as the wedding guest in a see-through dress, or the party girl who is really too plump for belly button jewelry—have their faces blotted out or their heads cut off.

The odd trio hits the road in the writer's '93 Toyota. "Cool," the shooters say to indicate approval. Should we stop here for gas? "Cool. Very cool." An old Chevy artfully rusting by the side of Route 66 is grist for their mill, and so is a cow poking its pale moist nose through a barbed-wire fence. The giant plastic steer outside an Ardmore steak house fascinates them, and they shoot it from all angles for ten minutes.

The film is developed and the travelogue edited. But a strange and wonderful thing happens: A sudden influx of advertising for the June issue creates a space problem, and something's got to give, and it's sure as hell not going to be the ad for Cleveland clubs or Spalding balls. So the following story never sees the light of day:

> On Sunday, June 10, you'll turn on your TV and watch Tiger or David or Phil win the U.S. Open on a long golf course with high rough, narrow fairways, and fast greens, and you'll have the feeling that you've seen it all before.
>
> But you haven't. Although the TV cameras at Southern Hills can't begin to capture it, golf in Oklahoma has a taste and smell completely unlike the eau de Oakmont we've become used to.
>
> It's a red dirt rural game north of the Red River, with oil derricks just over the fence and ceaseless prairie wind. The state is dotted with a measles rash of golf courses, most of them the misbegotten descendants of Oklahoma's sand green past. Southern Hills, they ain't. By the same token, two-KFC towns like Ardmore own venues suitable for an open, if not The Open.
>
> We traveled into the heart of the state, through limb-snapping ice storms, driving rain, and blessed sunshine. From Ada to Wewoka we searched for the essence of golf in the Tornado State. Nine hundred miles and three days later, we'd mulled a murder mystery, mystery meat, an eccentric duffer, and a golfing optometrist. We survived after one of our photographers placed his order in a deep country Subway by announcing, "I'm down with the six-inch tuna." And we believe we cracked the code. It seems the key to the game in Oklahoma is two dead guys.
>
> Dornick Hills Golf Club, Ardmore: A dozen deer nibbling the cold, wet grass of the club's front yard skitter away at the car's approach. And in the golf shop, the fawnlike assistant pro, Bradlea Cox, asks, "Ya'll want some coffee? We've got cookies, too." Oreos in a bowl.
>
> But Dornick Hills, no Bambi of a golf course, is the most subtly confounding sixty-four-hundred-yard track anywhere. "Charles Howell won the Maxwell

Invitational here in 1999 with a four under," says head pro Brad Martin. "The next week he wins the NCAA. Twenty-six under."

Most of the credit for the ingenious design goes to dead guy number one, the Father of Oklahoma Golf, Perry Duke Maxwell. Architects and architecture form the basis of many a golf in-crowd discussion, but you can hold your own with even the worst know-it-alls merely by uttering his name. Maxwell was a banker in Ardmore, an oil boomtown that for a time had the highest number of millionaires per capita in the country. A cultured man and a tennis aficionado—probably a baseliner—he took up golf in 1909 at age thirty and a few years later gave up banking in favor of designing courses. He crusaded against sand greens, the hallmark of the jackleg, we're-not-spending-any-money Oklahoma golf course. Which meant, until 1923, every "green" in the state.

"Darned if I know why he became a golf architect," says Jerry Westheimer, Sr., ninety-one, whose father-in-law, Dean Woods, built what Maxwell designed. "I never saw him actually play. He was a teetotaler, pretty religious, not much of a sense of humor. A Scotsman, you know."

We clamber up a slippery slope to a rocky plateau to the right of the seventh fairway and walk a bare dirt road that looks and clings like oily peanut butter, and there we contemplate the semicircle of stone arches above the grave of Perry Maxwell. Dodging cold raindrops dripping from a looming blackjack oak, the host pro explains that Dornick Hills, built in part on a dairy farm that Maxwell owned, was his first project, in 1913. Southern Hills (1935), the site of the 2001 Open, was among his last. He also redesigned Colonial in Fort Worth and Augusta National, so you know he had the goods. Maxwell's fame endures.

Not so Waco Turner, the other dead guy. Fifty years ago, oil millionaire Turner made Dornick Hills his home, and his Waco Turner Open was a PGA and LPGA event that briefly made Oklahoma golf famous. The tournament "has attained notice and prestige approaching that of the PGA Championship, the

USGA Open, and the Masters in the world of golf," wrote PGA president Horton Smith in the tournament program in 1953, stretching it a little. But now Waco Turner is gone and forgotten, even though he gave away a huge part of his fortune, usually a sure path to remembrance. Could his disappearance have something to do with the scandal of his wife's shooting? I mean, two gunshot wounds, and they ruled it a suicide.

Maxwell's monuments are everywhere in Oklahoma, but to find out more about the mysterious Waco Turner, we'll have to go to Burneyville.

The Eccentric Duffer, Fitzhugh: First we roll north on I-35 and then northeast on Highway 1 past Sulphur to look at Oak Hills, another Perry Maxwell design. But a decrepit sign above a seemingly bombed-out building in suburban Ada advertises . . . what? From the name and the pockmarked image of a snooty figure in plus-fours, it obviously has *something* to do with golf. We can't not stop.

We traverse half a mile of potholed road with railroad tracks on one side and rusting double-wides with goats in the front yard on the other. Then we discover a forlorn driving range and a nearly hidden and haphazard par 3 course, its dirt road entrance chained and locked. We circumnavigate the place in a vain attempt to locate the clubhouse. All we find is more grim-looking real estate, and a house with a Bible verse, something from Philippians, spray-painted on the plywood backboard of the driveway basketball hoop.

Perhaps the Eccentric Duffer lives within.

Oak Hills, Ada: With the eerie rumble of a runaway train, a tornado crept up on Oak Hills last spring. The funnel stayed mostly airborne over Ada, home of East Central Oklahoma University. But at ten before eight that morning, it came to ground on a house next to the first fairway. There went the house. It rumbled and sucked its way across the first fairway, and the ninth fairway, and there went some trees and the sand in the bunkers. On toward the cart barn . . . and then the whirling cloud ascended again, saving Oak Hills's insurer a major damage claim but depriving us of a flying golf cart story.

"Maxwell designed most of the holes here," says Erin Bevil, one of several members of the ECOU Tigers golf team who are practice putting when we arrive. Their golf bags and windshirts are black and orange. "This course is never ranked in the state's top ten but it definitely should be." Oak Hills demonstrates two of the great man's trademarks: a couple of tees that aim you straight toward trouble instead of straight down the fairway, and rolling, tumbling greens, "Maxwell waves," to compensate for the flat ground he usually had to work with.

Bevil and the other lads share a similar pride in East Central golf, but their most famous alum has all the sizzle of an optometrist. In fact, he was an optometrist—Senior PGA Tour star Dr. Gil Morgan. You may remember Gil from such Tour wins as the Glen Campbell–Los Angeles Open, the Danny Thomas–Memphis Classic, and the Joe Garagiola–Tucson Open. Gil's from Wewoka, about an hour up the road. Photographer John Look says he's always wanted to see Wewoka. So to Wewoka we will go.

Wewoka Municipal Golf Course: The town is just as small as you'd think, and the golf course is the kind of dog track Perry Maxwell tried to stamp out. Built by bored oilmen in 1949, it features nine Wonder Bra greens, small, pushed up and hard to hold. But Gil developed the feather touch to hold 'em.

"Gil was a great athlete," recalls John Norman, a high-school teammate who is, like his daddy before him, the pharmacist at Norman Drug in Wewoka. "He played quarterback, and was on the baseball team, but his golf, well. . . . After high school, I went to pharmacy school, and he went to East Central. In the NAIA tournament, I shot my usual 75, then I look at the leader board and see 'Gil Morgan, 66.' I'd never heard of him breaking 80. Someone said there was only one explanation: Bobby Jones had died and come back in Gil's body."

Norman is a world traveler by Wewoka standards, so

we asked him what makes golf in Oklahoma different, if anything. Others had said wind and weather set the state apart, but Norman detects an economic difference. "It's cheap," he says. "I just got back from Big Horn [in Palm Desert, California], and the green fee was three hundred dollars. Here, it's thirty dollars. A month."

Tommy Bolt, Haworth: We didn't actually go to the southeast corner of the state to see the ancestral home of Mr. Bolt. We just called him at his home in Florida.

The last time the U.S. Open came to Oklahoma, in 1958, "Thunder" Bolt won at Southern Hills. "Nah, they didn't make a big deal out of me being from Oklahoma," he says. "I was born there, but my mother died when I was two and half, and we moved to Shreveport, Louisiana." But the press often identified the Open champ as "Oklahoma's terrible-tempered Tommy Bolt," so the state and his angry mental state have been linked in the public mind.

But nowadays Bolt says he's had just about enough. "I threw a couple of clubs and got credit for throwin' all of them," he says. "Everybody's thrown a club but you don't read about anybody else. Now think about that."

Cushing Country Club: Dazed from the road, and disappointed that foul weather has kept us from playing any Oklahoma golf, we crawl out of the minivan and see an unfamiliar sight: our shadows. Pro Glen Rose invites us to play a few holes in return for saying something nice about Cushing CC, the third-oldest (1921) course in the state. Done. The prolific and ubiquitous Perry Maxwell designed the greens.

Some club pros in the petroleum belt refer to their in-the-business members as "oilies." The man who takes care of the carts at Cushing, Virgil Bradley, seventy-three, is an Oily, Second Class. He used to work at the refinery on the outskirts of town. "Feed stock, low-grade gas, diesel fuel, slurry, butane, propane," says Bradley, looking comfortable behind the wheel of an E Z Go, reciting some of the exciting products the plant produced. "Kerosene, naphtha, gasoline blends, Platformate . . ."

We stop at the spooky, long-abandoned Hudson Oil Refinery on our way out of Cushing. Its rusting pipes and towers might make a perfect backdrop for the final scene of an action thriller, when Clint Eastwood and the bad guy have their final confrontation.

Hick'ry House Bar-B-Q, Marietta: On Wednesdays and Wednesdays only, you can get the special baked potato at Fred and Freda Walker's restaurant on Highway 32 West. Thick strips of beef hide among the usual spud additives. It will hold you until dinner.

Falconhead Resort and Country Club, Burneyville: Finally, we catch up with the second dead man, Waco Franklin Turner. He must have been a handful. When he finally got to be too much for the other oil millionaires at Dornick Hills, he went a little ways south and east and built his own place. At Turner Lodge and Country Club (now Falconhead), the part Waco Indian former schoolteacher was free to continue the unique customs of his tournament and to institute a few more. For example, he'd carry a burlap sack full of cash to the eighteenth green and give it away to the players as they finished their rounds. You got $15 for each birdie, $25 for a chip-in, $500 for an eagle, the same for the low round of the day, and $2,500 for a hole-in-one. Cash on the barrelhead. For the hell of it, one year he gave Byron Nelson a palomino (which turned out to be mean-tempered) on the first tee. Babe Zaharias asked, "Where's mine?" at the first of the two LPGA tournaments the Turners held, so crazy Waco gave her a golden horse, too. He always watched the play from behind the wheel of a new Cadillac, which he drove anywhere he damn well pleased, even across fairways.

Cocktail hour was an important ritual for Waco. "At three o'clock in the afternoon I like to get me a jug of bourbon and a jug of water and sit down and drink them and not have nobody bother me," he told an

> interviewer. "I stay in about an hour or so. That's restful." His wife Opie fortified herself with similar gusto for many years, which to some gives credence to the "suicide" explanation of her death in 1962—even though she had the two bullet holes in her side. Of course, some people whispered that Waco shot Opie. We'll never know. But we do know they had no children, he called her "Mama," and they spent or gave away every penny of the $50 million they found in the ground. Nobody built a statue or named a bridge for them, even though some say Waco did more for Oklahoma golf than any other ten men.
>
> As we drove the long miles to the airport at the end of the trip, we had plenty of time to think about the two fathers of the game in the heart of the oil patch. We decided that both men would be remembered more clearly, and more fondly, if only Perry Maxwell had a little more Waco Turner in him. And Waco a little more Perry.

Howell's homecoming gets off to a lousy start. On Tuesday morning, before his second practice round, he picks up the *Oklahoma City Daily Oklahoman*. He reads MCVEIGH EXECUTED, the headline on page one. He turns to sports. FOLLOW THE TIGER is the head over the lead story. "For much of the day, it was an aimless crowd of thirty-five thousand," reports Mac Bentley. "That all changed at midafternoon, however, when Woods showed up . . ." In the far left column, Charles reads his own name in a headline: HOWELL HAS LOOSE LIPS, FAT WALLET. *What?* He'd had, he thought, a pleasant chat with columnist John Rohde the day before. He ate a club sandwich in the big white hilltop clubhouse at Southern Hills while Rohde asked questions about a variety of subjects—what has your first year on the Tour been like, what's up with you and Heather, are you looking forward to this, your first major championship? And what about turning pro a year ago—any regrets about that?

"Charles Howell said he should have known better," Rohde wrote.

"But it's tough to know better when you don't know much."

The Dutch Uncle column takes Howell to task for turning pro in the summer of 2000, three weeks after his record-setting 23 under par in the NCAA, and three weeks after saying he'd be back next year, "leaving a hole the size of Augusta in the Cowboys program." Without Howell, noted Rohde, Oklahoma State didn't win any tournaments and didn't make the cut at the NCAA, the result being that Charles's "name has pretty much been Dirt."

Feeling deceived, Howell hails the columnist outside the locker room and asks him what the hell? How could anyone question his pursuit of the dream he'd had since he was seven years old? And he's won $365,000 in official money this year, over $636,000 total in less than a year as a pro—doesn't that prove he was ready to make a living from the game? Besides, who was hurt? Not the university—golf is not a revenue sport. Howell thinks it's plain that Mike Holder figuratively whispered in Rohde's ear when he wrote this column. The Oklahoma State coach owns an enviable record both for winning big events and for seeing to it that his players graduate, and by turning pro after his junior year, Howell hurt Holder in both areas. The column feels like payback to its subject, and looks like a writer ingratiating himself to a source.

Twenty-four hours later, however, Howell is impressively not bitter. It's the day before the U.S. Open and he's not going to think about much but how to shoot a low score at Southern Hills. Moreover, he's decided that his first major piece of negative press is a rite of passage, part of the fire walk for a top player. It reminds him of an incident at the Memorial, when he walked onto the practice tee and said to Bambi, "I'm a jerk."

"What?" asked caddie Ron "Bambi" Levin.

"I just signed forty-nine autographs," Howell said. "The fiftieth one in line called me a jerk for not signing her hat."

Nothing happened in Howell's life for a long time except golf, golf, golf, and studying at the kitchen table precisely two-and-a-half hours a night. Then personal and professional milestones fell like dominoes. As a sophomore in college, he dated for the first time. Fell in love for the first time. Won the NCAA by an unprecedented margin with a record low score. Three weeks later, he finished second in a Buy.com event in Greensboro—which would have paid him $35,200 if he had been a pro. So he turned pro. Got an agent. Signed a big contract with Callaway. Won a quarter of a million in half a year. Summoned unexpectedly to Q School Stage 2, he failed. Then he won sufficient money in a seven-tournament sudden death to play the Tour the rest of the year. He's about to close on a house in Orlando—the better to be near his instructor, David Leadbetter. And he and Heather moved their marriage date dramatically forward, from December to next week, right after the Open. All this in about a year and a half.

In his rapid ascension up golf's ladder, Howell's life has

been remarkably similar to Tiger's. The big difference is Charles's commitment to one woman, while Woods continues to look around (Tiger will eventually pair up with a Nordic beauty named Elin Nordegren, Jesper Parnevik's nanny).

Howell still needs to win another hundred thousand dollars or so to secure his playing privileges for 2002, but with a barefoot wedding on the beach in Maui just days away, there's no way he'll have the focus to crack an egg at Southern Hills. So you scan the practice tee to look for someone else to challenge Tiger, who hits ball after ball with a pronounced left-to-right flight, presumably on purpose. There are a lot of guys to like. There's Davis Love III with his swing describing two huge circles, one with his hands, one with the head of his club. Duval looks like he's killing the ball, and he's finished in the top ten of the last three U.S. Opens. Mickelson gives the lie to the myth that all left-handed swings are beautiful, but the way he plays majors you've got to give him a chance. There's another big guy, Tom Lehman, one of the two or three best at hitting the center of the ball with the center of his club. The smart money's on Lehman, he plays great here, and he looks great, having lost a lot of weight since we saw him last. He says he did it for his wife, Melissa, not for Tiger. Nick Faldo's grinding away, his shirt soaked with sweat, and he's reunited with his caddie from his glory days, Fanny Sunneson. Blond Billy Mayfair, with his wacky swing and his I-made-a-deal-with-the-Devil putting stroke could be a contender. Couldn't he?

No. He's too short off the tee. And Love has a stiff neck

and Lehman can't make a putt and Faldo's time has passed and there must be some reason why neither Duval nor Mickelson has won a major. On the day before the U.S. Open, everyone looks a little fretful and slightly unworthy. For it's been a full year since anyone but Eldrick T. Woods has won one of the four biggest championships, a thoroughly rare, almost unprecedented domination. "You look at Duval and Mickelson, and you know they never had a doubt that they'd be number one in the world," says Brandel Chamblee, a veteran of fourteen years on the Tour. "Then they had to get used to the idea that they may never be."

But have David and Phil and the others gone from acceptance to resignation all the way to . . . perversity? Are they eager victims enjoying the spanking a little bit, like those bank employees in Stockholm? In the summer of 1973 a couple of greedy Swedish morons held up the *Kreditbanken*, and botched the job, and ended up taking four people hostage. At the end of a six-day ordeal, the former hostages not only refused to testify against their captors, they raised money for their defense. One or two of them even became interested romantically in the armed robbers.

For us to conclude that big-time golf suffers from Stockholm Syndrome, four conditions would have to apply. First, does the abuser—Tiger—threaten the victim's survival? Well, no, but he certainly damages their image of themselves as golf champions. Second, is the victim isolated? "Insulated" is more like it. Touring pros live in courtesy cars, in airports, and on golf courses, mostly cut off from real life. Third, is the victim unable to escape? Escape is not a problem on the PGA Tour. You can always take a week off. A lot of players take pains to enter the tournaments that Tiger doesn't. Escaping from the knowledge that he's much better than you, however, is less easily done. And fourth, does the captor show his victims some occasional kindness? Yes. Tiger says hi. And no, like Nicklaus, he *never* lets up on the golf course.

The Tiger Syndrome is a powerful thing, but golf is filled with feats of glory performed by guys who were too competitive or too unaware to surrender in the face of superior talent. Ben Hogan owned the most intimidating combination of skill and personality in golf history, but the angels landed on Herman Keiser at the Masters in '46 and on Jack Fleck at the U.S. Open in '55, and both beat the Hawk. Twice Tiger has been involved in similar dramas. At the PGA in 2000, a little guy with a bad back and an unusual swing just would not quit, and it took a record low score, a playoff, and a piece of lottery winner's luck for Woods to finally beat Bob May.

An even funnier swing and a truly hilarious grip conquered Woods once, back in '96. It was only the Quad City Classic, but it was Tiger's first time in contention as a pro and fans and the media hung on the outcome like it was a presidential election. The winner in an upset was Edward Ray Fiori of Sugarland, Texas. Eddie Ray on a PGA Tour practice tee looks like a '63 Corvair in a Rolls Royce showroom. On the practice tee at the Nelson, tall, athletic Vijay Singh paused from making elegant swings to observe the man hitting next to him. He looked at Ed Fiori's gut, the sweat on his too-tight shirt accenting his belly button cavern, his hands on his club like two garter snakes in love, the orthopedic device on his left elbow, and the swing in which he did not fully transfer his weight, resulting in cut shots of unimpressive length. "I cannot believe we're in the same tournament," sighed Singh.

But Fiori chips and putts like the devil when he's on and he beat Tiger at Quad Cities in '96. He didn't know he couldn't. Not that "The Grip" wants to talk about it much now. His comments about the great day are perfunctory and few. Asked if his big win changed his life, and how, he says, "Oh, yeah. Lots of guys like you ask me about it."

This U.S. Open field must have a Keiser, Fleck, or Fiori in it, an opportunist whom chance will infuse with dumb luck and smart decisions. You poll such pundits as you can find around the practice tee. Agent Nancy Cain of Gaylord Sports tips one of her clients, Rocco Mediate. Writer Cameron Morfit of *Maximum Golf* likes Frank Lickliter. Earlier in the day, Frank agreed to play Twenty Questions for the September issue of the magazine he loves. He and his elfin interviewer took off their sunglasses.

Q: Favorite food group?
A: Meat.

"He was way into it," Morfit says. "He's a man's man, with lots of charisma, very cool. He likes to live large, totally a *Maximum Golf* guy."

Dan Strimple, an instructor instructing an unfamiliar young man hitting balls next to Tiger, shrugs when you ask if his guy has a chance. "As good a chance as anyone else," he says, a deep statement about the vicissitudes of golf or a deliberate lie, since his student seems to be having trouble getting his three wood airborne. The young chap failing to keep his weight back at impact is named Clark Dennis. He is not chopped liver—Dennis tied for sixth in the Open at Oakmont in 1994, and he won $401,000 on the PGA Tour in 1998 before dropping off the map in 2000. But he has no place in the popular mind. Dennis therefore exemplifies the U.S. Open myth, that anyone can get in, and anyone can win. So *Sports Illustrated* has sent one of its best writers, Michael Bamberger, to hang with him this week, and perhaps chronicle a Cinderella story.

The players on the practice tee tinker and tweak their swings in a final rehearsal, their shirts and belt lines drenched with sweat from humidity and worry. It's plain that whoever plans to challenge Tiger this week will have to be in great shape, because the hills at Southern Hills seem to trap the heat like the walls of a sauna.

"HEY, TIGER, YOU WANT A BEER?"

Bob and Kim's place fits like a glove into a high southern hill on the outer rim of Tulsa. Ornately tangled limbs of live oak trees, lit from the base at night, put a visitor in an appropriately dreamy mood before entering this dream house. Inside, it's all horizontal lines, exposed and polished cedar beams and sheets of glass. In the back there's an ingenious complex of wooden decks, whose topmost level, soaring at treetop height at the top of twenty narrow stairs, is an eight-person crow's nest. From there you look down at the azure rectangle of the pool or out at the twinkling lights of the city, miles away and hundreds of feet below.

Tiger's renting the house next door.

"Tiger, you suck!"

For several nights during Open week, a witty assemblage takes turns calling out into the warm night air to the next-door neighbor, an unseen presence behind a high hedge and a thick stand of trees. Here's the host, Bob, who made a million when he sold Million Air, his jet fueling and maintenance company. Meet Bob's beautiful wife, Kim, a massage therapist, and their one-year-old son, Noah. And this is Les, who has been selling Tulsa life insurance for thirty years, and his date Cyndi, the owner of a wicked sense of humor and a landscape design company. Joining them are Dan the golf pro and Gaylen the lawyer. Both of the latter are from out of town, and both will have another beer, thank you. But they're part of Clark Dennis's support group, and Clark tees off at 6:40 in the first round tomorrow morning, so they can't stay out too late.

The Tulsans are exhilarated to have the U.S. Open in town. And to have the best-known player in the world not fifty yards away and the close associates of the least-known competitor in the Open right here dipping celery stalks in the onion dip, well, it's just too cool. Kim volunteers that yesterday she'd seen Woods in the 10 Items Or Less checkout at the Albertson's grocery store down at the bottom of the hill on Yale and Eighty-fifth. Kim selected her balsamic vinegar and baby formula and moments later went through the same line, and the cashier whispered excitedly that Tiger had been "so nice" and had purchased bubble gum.

His brand preference—either Bubblicious or Dubbl Bubbl—went unnoticed in the excitement. Then he got in the front passenger-side door of a black Suburban with heavily tinted windows and went back up the hill.

From Bob and Kim's suburban perch, Tulsa looks like the interior of a vast fort or castle, rimmed by hills like battlements. Bob points out some landmarks: That water tower, looking like a ball teed up for a giant to hit, is called golf ball hill. That's the Arkansas River snaking through the city and next to it—see the plane?—is Riverside Airport, a small private field. The bright lights belong to Cityplex Tower, and across the street is the Prayer Tower and the rest of Oral Roberts University. Southern Hills is on past ORU to the north but you can't see it.

Like everything existing only in time, the city's historic landmarks are harder to see. The town's name derived from *tallasi,* Creek Indian for "old town," the root word for both Tallahassee and Tulsa. Our federal government had marched the Creeks out of their ancestral land in Alabama and into the northeast quadrant of present-day Oklahoma in the 1830s. Their traditional enemies—the Seminoles, Chickasaws, and Cherokee—were forced to join the Creeks in the new Indian Nation. The displaced people tried to get their lives restarted but it was complicated, in part because whites infiltrated, many of them with black slaves. Interracial marriage was common, which was likely when and where Earl Woods of nearby Manhattan, Kansas, acquired his white and American Indian ancestors.

The Civil War was a disaster for all the tribes in the Indian Territory. Tribal leaders backed the wrong side, and their alliances with the Confederacy led to a complex series of raids, retaliation, and defection. Long story short, the war and its aftermath resulted in continued, organized defrauding of the Native Americans. Their big disadvantage was that they had always lived communal lives, and didn't fully grasp the concept of private property. So to a large extent, the Oklahoma Indians lost their land again.

Land that became worth a hell of a lot more than they ever dreamed half a century later, thanks to oil. Cushing, forty miles east of Tulsa, had one of the biggest early strikes, thanks to the luck and perseverance of Tom "Dry Hole" Slick, an oil prospector with a career batting average up to then of .000. Within months of his big hit in March 1912, the Oklahoma economy was transformed, leading to such as crazy Waco Turner, and to Perry Maxwell.

Despite its height, you can't see Greenwood Street from Bob and Kim's deck. It's not much of a landmark anyway, not the kind of place anyone wants to illuminate. Time and a conspiracy of silence further dim the events of May 31, 1921, when Tulsa hosted the worst race riot in U.S. history. That night, after a humid day with temperatures of about 90 degrees, whites systematically looted and burned practically every house on Greenwood, the center of the city's black community. Why did Tulsa, of all places, harbor such racial hatred?

The what is more easily told than the why. After the morning Memorial Day parade, business returned to normal in Tulsa, which meant that Dick Rowland was shining shoes in the lobby of the Drexel Building on Main Street. Rowland was nineteen, black, and he had to go to the bathroom. Since no blacks were allowed to use the public facilities, he had to go to an upper floor to access the lousy cubicle reserved for people of color. The elevator operator was Sarah Page, seventeen, white, and screaming—that on their ascent, Rowland had assaulted her. He was arrested the next day. The newspapers covered the case on their front pages, speculating in print about the chances for a lynching.

To prevent that, seventy-five to a hundred black men surrounded the jail, most of them armed, most of them World War I veterans who'd marched in the parade the day before. About fifteen hundred whites coalesced around them. Insults were exchanged, then gunfire. Twelve people fell bleeding. When the whites were unable to get Rowland out of his cell, they headed for Greenwood Street, stopping along the way to break into hardware stores and pawn shops for guns and ammunition. Mayor T. D. Evans appointed special deputies to control the situation until the National Guard arrived, but the deputies interpreted their duty to be to round up and detain black men, men who might have defended Greenwood Street.

In *Tulsa! Biography of the American City*, author Danney Goble provides precise numbers of homes burned to the foundation (1,115) and houses robbed of everything (563) and people requiring treatment for gunshot wounds (184 black, 48 white). "There were no official death totals (presumably because officials had no earthly idea)," Goble writes. "But informed estimates ran anywhere from fifty-five to three hundred. Even now, nobody knows."

Almost no one was punished. Sarah Page didn't file charges against Dick Rowland, and both left Tulsa for good. But the town did not hang its head in shame; in fact, within weeks, a vigorous branch of the Ku Klux Klan began life on the edge of Greenwood Street. The new Klavern bought a creaky Methodist church, razed it, and built in its place the largest assembly hall in the state, capacity three thousand. They called it Beno Hall. As in be no blacks, unionists, Catholics, or Jews allowed.

Eighty years later, Beno be no more, Tulsa is one of the coolest, most progressive cities in the Southwest, and a mostly black man sleeps in a house on its nicest southern hill. And the whole world waits to see what he'll do tomorrow.

> CAN ANYONE TAKE DOWN TIGER? THE US OPEN TODAY 12:00 P.M. ET *ESPN* A COSMIC CONVERGENCE Tiger's otherworldly play is no surprise to early mentors
>
> —Headlines from the front of *USA Today* Sports Section, June 14

Tiger's greatest rival walks on the wrong side of the ropes. A year ago, at Pebble Beach, Gary Nicklaus's father had announced his retirement from the U.S. Open. So after forty-four consecutive appearances, and four wins, this is Jack's first time to just watch since the Open came to his home course in Columbus, Scioto, when he was kid. He gets into it. With his pristine white shoes and a patterned navy blue silk shirt, and his familiar intensity undiminished by the fact that he has an umbrella in his hands and not a golf club, Jack looks ready to play himself.

At 7:00 A.M., forty minutes before Gary tees off in the company of Howell and Chris Smith, Jack stands in the instructor's pose behind Gary on the practice tee. David Leadbetter performs the same function for Howell. No one deconstructs or criticizes: This is confidence-building time. "That looks good," they both say. "That looks very good." (Strimple had already performed this function for Dennis, who is already on the second hole. And Butch Harmon would speak no evil for Tiger before he got started at 12:30.)

As you know from shaking his hand, Gary has his father's sincere smile, blue eyes, and small, calloused hands. He also has his dad's nonclassic lift of the right elbow on the backswing. But Gary wraps his hands around his neck on the follow-through while Jack finished with his hands up by his left ear. He hits, Jack watches, and the tension builds. Gary needs a good tournament: He hasn't won much money this year.

The early Thursday morning breeze feels pleasant and the temperature is tolerable, and the gray sky presages rain. Despite the company and the glory of the event, however, watching this Open is not fun. For as you duck and dodge in the Nicklaus-Howell-Smith gallery it becomes immediately clear that Perry Maxwell did not have a gallery in mind when he designed Southern Hills. The place feels like downtown Boston, filled with one-way streets and dead ends. They've roped the second hole so that if you walk down the right side you can't get to the third. The blend of hummocks and mature oaks makes it hard to walk and difficult to see, and the minimal number of greenside grassy knolls makes it hard to rest, unless you can find a grandstand seat. One of the few such half-amphitheaters belongs to the eighteenth, but a complicated series of roped barriers and stolid marshals reduce access and egress to a trickle. If you're not careful around eighteen, you may find yourself immobilized for long minutes in a human bottleneck, like a Tokyo commuter in a mob scene in *Godzilla*. But how could Maxwell have known in 1935 that this oilman's course would host a U.S. Open, or how big the Open would be, or the number of people golf's stars would attract?

Jack and Barbara Nicklaus concentrate intently on their son, while a small group concentrates intently on them. Gary's parents sip from identical royal blue bottles of water and march resolutely together from greens to tees and up the fairway. The hair on their two heads is the same mix of brown, blond, and gray, and they've even come to resemble each other facially, as couples who've been together for a long time sometimes do. After a few holes of furtive observation, it occurs to you how ridiculous it is to watch someone watch someone, even if it is Jack Nicklaus. Still, you sneak a peek on the fourteenth, a par 3 with a tiny plateau of a green, when Gary hits his tee shot in a bunker eight steps from the flagstick and then *shanks* it coming out. He's hit golf's worst shot, a sickening little lateral dead right. Jack is stoic. Gary is furious but composes himself and chips the next one up close.

No one in this group plays particularly well. Howell impresses with his ball striking, but his putting is not worthy. On the 534-yard par 5 thirteenth, for example, he shows that he's in Tiger's class by driving his ball very long into a very tight fairway. While Nicklaus and Smith flounder around in the woods, Howell and Bambi select a four iron for his next one over a figure-eight-shaped pond and between two bunkers. He hits another perfect shot to twenty feet. "Charles! Yeah!" yell two dozen or so young people wearing Oklahoma State orange. But their hero proves he is not Tiger by jamming his first putt four feet past, and lipping out the next one, and then not reacting very much. He shoots 75.

After clambering up the steep hill leading to the clubhouse at the final hole, and watching his son hole out for an eight-over-par 78, eighteen media representatives encircle Jack Nicklaus. He stands near the tenth tee under a hackberry tree with a view of the golf course behind him, a great shot for the cameraman from Channel 12 NBC in Tulsa. He listens to a dozen questions, eight of them inane—"What's it like, watching your son?"—and answers each without a hint of mockery or sarcasm.

While Jack's jury surrounds him like he's a Maypole, the media setup for the players recalls a trendy night club, with those few deemed cool enough to enter the club (the players) on this side of thirty feet of metal fence, and the numerous not-cool-enoughs (the media) on that side. An hour before, Clark Dennis, angry after a 79, had uttered a phrase that got widely used—with a bit of editing—in the nation's newspapers the next day: "I only wish everyone had to play through the shit we had to play through," he said, referring both to the early morning wind and to the very early morning.

Howell's postround chat goes better than Jack's or Clark's. Affable and smiling despite his highest score of the year, he walks through media row and talks to anybody who wants to talk to him. This takes about half an hour. "I did what I was supposed to do except I hit the lips instead of the bottoms," he says. "We'll get bigger holes tomorrow. . . . What did I learn? How good a score par is at Southern Hills, and at the U.S. Open. . . . Pressure? We're kinda getting used to it. . . . No, having Jack watch didn't add any pressure or bother me in the least. Gary and I are good friends and Jack's always been real positive with me. But I'm sure he wanted to get inside the ropes a couple of times and just help Gary." Howell's remarks won't make anyone forget—or look up—Edward R. Murrow. But each interviewer thanks him when he's done like he just bought dinner, because he makes everyone feel comfortable and because he's trying. Maybe the prospect of marrying the beautiful girl from Kingfisher on a beach in Maui next week has put a little extra zip in his lip.

Brandel Chamblee's another guy who always acts like there's something to be happy about. Let's see, his wife, the former Karen Medina, looks like Mary Tyler Moore in her prime, perhaps better. His four-year-old son Brandel, Jr., wants to be a pirate. They all live in a big house in Scottsdale, and he plays golf for a living . . . why, yes, there is cause to smile. His 72 is a respectable score on this day, on this course, and he's happy to help fill up notebooks and videotape as he passes through the media gauntlet. "Yeah, 72, pretty good," Chamblee says. With his soothing voice, his speech devoid of ums and ahs, and his brain in harmony with his tongue, Chamblee has the TV boys asking him to come up to the booth and talk to the folks watching at home. He doesn't do it much. It smacks too much of retirement to him and at forty-one, that's not a topic he cares to consider. He'd like to talk instead about his hybrid two iron, a club he calls Pat, after the ambisexual character of the same name on *Saturday Night Live*. "You can't tell if it's a girl or a boy," he says, or an iron or a wood. "Uh-oh, look out."

Fat sprinkles splatter the concrete and asphalt on the hill outside the locker room. The TV crews and most of the writers run for the giant media center farther up the hill, past the pool and beyond the clubhouse. As the raindrops become sticks on a snare drum, and then a hundred snare drums, the players and caddies duck into the locker room, there to be joined by more and more participants as they come in off the course, each one wetter than the one before. Soon the humidity escaping from their bodies and the smoke from the cigarettes of the smokers who gather not near enough to the door—Jim McGovern, Tim Herron, Willie Wood, and Thongchai Jaidee—forms a gray wash of indoor smog.

An hour passes and the rain beats down with a hypnotic sound, which causes lots of the inmates to fall silent and stare blankly at the old wooden lockers. A few small groups quietly tell each other stories. Players and caddies tend to equipment and clothes. Up a short staircase and to the right is an informal dining room with round tables for six that are now seating ten but there's a guard at the door reminding you that this room is for contestants and their families only. So the miscellaneous fringe players sit in the narrow aisles on skinny locker-room benches, even on the floor. Someone's ordered pizza, and cardboard boxes marked Mazzio's circulate up and down the aisles like communion plates.

Several idle minds play Name That Twin. Q: Who is today's Sam Snead? A: Ernie Els. Bobby Jones? Justin Leonard. Like Justin, Jones would have worn Polo. Bruce Crampton equals David Duval—similar graceful swing, same look when you ask a stupid question, same second-place finish in the majors. Johnny Miller? Charles Howell—skinny former nerds with big swings and big games. Frank Stranahan and Keith Clearwater, both weightlifters who look like leading men. Hogan? For his precision and his two U.S. Opens, Lee Janzen, maybe, although he's far from a perfect fit. Fred Couples gets actor David Duchovny. Stuart Appleby and actor Troy Donahue. Tiger and . . . Tiger and . . . but Tiger has no twin.

Another half hour passes in the circa 1935 dark wood and white paint room. Someone opens the door for a moment and the water splashing off the roof onto the sidewalk sounds like a cow's micturition in a concrete stall. When the rain lets up a bit you say "excuse me" to two dozen people and squeeze out the exit to look for a scoreboard. It costs you a wet neck and shoulders but you stand there for a moment staring at WOODS, T. +3. He'd played only nine holes before the midafternoon deluge, so his uncomfortable relationship to par may not mean much. He shot 40 on the first nine at the '97 Masters, after all. But still, it looks funny to see him six shots behind Hale Irwin, who'd just celebrated his fifty-sixth birthday.

In time, the USGA bows to the inevitable and cancels

play for the day, knowing it will cost them untold logistical problems tomorrow, and probably on Saturday.

Late in the day, the sun comes out for a few minutes, too late to help the tournament, but perfect for the *Sports Illustrated* photographer who needs to shoot Clark Dennis and his family back at the Doubletree Hotel. They've been instructed to look casual, as if they might be about to go swimming. So Clark and his lovely wife, Vicki, and their oldest son, Will, meet Bamberger and the photographer by the indoor pool, where U.S. Open contestant Esteban Toledo is trying to teach his two-year-old daughter Eden to swim. She's got pink inflatable things on her arms but each time Daddy lets her go, she shrieks so pure a sound you want to check your glasses for fractures.

THE HALF OF THE FIELD that didn't complete its first round has to return very early on Friday to finish. Although the rain is gone the heat returns. It enervates the players and their walking audience, catching them between the vapor escaping from the ground and the big heat lamp above, like waiting fast food. Applause is muted or nonexistent. Sullen, listless, incomplete, this Open still waits for a first-round leader in the afternoon of its second day, and it waits for Tiger to do something. It gets one but not the other. Retief Goosen, 66, and Tiger Woods, 74. "It's Goosen," the thirty-one-year-old South African tells the media. "Goose with an N." He's soft spoken and polite, with Dutch-accented English. You'd cast him as the son of the owner of the diamond mine.

Woods rises from his bed in the house on the hill at 4:30 and is on the tenth green, ready to tap in for par, at 6:55. His mom's watching, wearing a black and orange Tiger-themed outfit. You hope she didn't hear that shameful "Tiger sucks" remark. A horn sounds at 7:04, the signal to resume. Tiger, Thomas Björn, and Jeff Quinney play their eight and three-quarters holes in three hours, break for half an hour, then go out for eighteen more. Other schedules are worse. Jeff Freeman, for example, a pro from Norman, Oklahoma, had hit his drive into the eighteenth fairway when the rain-delay horn sounded at 3:39 on Thursday. He returned to the course on Friday before dawn, hit a few balls, then played his half a hole. He signed his card at 7:15 and puzzled over what to do next, because his second round wouldn't start until 5:00 P.M. Other late Friday starters like Dennis and Chamblee hang around their hotel rooms and the practice tee with the uneasy feeling of messed-up routines, and with uncertainty that they will be finished before dark. This will be an exhausting day for everyone.

And the heat goes on. But the blessed refreshment of refrigerated air fills the cavernous white press tent, which stays very full throughout the event. A new reporter remembers his surprise and disappointment when meeting Bob Green over a decade ago in a similar facility. Not that the Associated Press golf writer was anything but a gentleman, but because his face was so pale and his arms were pearly white. The obvious conclusion: He didn't actually see the great shots by Watson, Miller, and Nicklaus he described in his tournament stories. He saw them on TV, or relied on eyewitnesses who were not himself. And what with more and better television coverage, and laptops, looming deadlines—and the day's notable players coming to them, instead of the reverse—many writers cover a golf tournament without ever seeing the golf course, much less the key shot, no matter what the weather. Staying inside is more efficient, less work, and the bathroom's out this door and the food's out that door.

In the crossroads of the media center you say howdy to such as Tommy Bolt, the 1958 Open champ right here at Southern Hills. Bolt, eighty-three, and dressed like it's '73, gives you the big grin and a "how-ya-doin'-pal-great-to-see-ya," his chin outthrust like FDR's. Bolt's a hoot, but Robert Trent Jones, Jr., is an education. He's the son of a brand name, the man who invented golf course architecture in the United States. And, according to the title of a story in the tournament program, his father was "The Man Who MADE the Open." You could argue that Ben Hogan "made" the U.S. Open in this sense, that is, he popularized it and defined it. At any rate, the two came famously together in 1951 when the USGA hired Jones to toughen that year's Open course, Oakland Hills. He did his job so well that the players who are still alive who played that week are still bitching. Did his job so well that Hogan won. And Robert Trent Jones became "the Open Doctor." Nine courses that he designed or remodeled hosted fourteen Opens, and one of the courses he tweaked was Southern Hills. He said something back in Hogan's heyday that the USGA agreed with: The game, Jones said, "had outrun architecture."

Both Trent Jones's sons followed him into this curious profession. There's no analogous job in any other sport, since most other games standardize their playing fields into rectangles, squares, circles, or baseball's piece of pie. But golf remakes itself a little bit with each new course. Sometimes grandly, sometimes not—the results depend as much on the client as on the designer. Like Jim Furyk's backswing, the men playing god with golf are composed of four parts: salesman, artist, engineer, and sportsman. Each of the four-parted architects have one big problem: To many people, the game has again outrun its architecture. If this is true, Tiger has outrun the farthest.

Robert Trent Jones, Jr.—"please call me Bob"—has some thoughts on this and a dozen other issues. He's sixty-three, beetle-browed and professorial with his lank, longish hair and a look of amused intelligence, like he's just recalled the punchline of a damn good joke the poet Petrarch told the pope back in the fourteenth century. "I'm a Democrat, so the Woods family bringing these different cultures together has been very interesting to me," says Jones. "From his mother's side, there's the pleasantness of the Thai people, who have this saying: 'Bend with the wind.' They bend with the wind and they've never been conquered. And to that you add the military approach of Tiger's father.

"I wrote Tiger a letter when he was fourteen—something about how to read a golf course and a way to look at the strength or difficulty of bunkers—and was pleased to find out that he kept that letter on a table next to his bed.

"We've built a lot of golf courses in the Far East and

I've been very deeply influenced by the spirituality of their culture. So I might understand a little of his Asian side. One of Tiger's strengths is that he doesn't care what people think of him. He already knows he's all right. That's from his mother. Many people in golf wear masks, hiding their true inner selves, their fearful or troubled sides, their vulnerability. Then they become prone to gamesmanship or to not revealing any emotion, like Hogan. But Tiger seems to have no mask—perhaps because he has no fear. He may have Earl to thank for that."

Yes, Jones says, he's designing golf courses that are longer than any he's done in the past. Golf architects do not bend with the wind. "You'll notice that the game has always been filled with war metaphors," he says above the deep hum of the air-conditioner compressors. "Holes were named for battles or battlefields—such as The Redan [a par three at North Berwick in Scotland], which was a fortress at Sebastopol in the Crimean War. And look what happened at Augusta National. Gene Sarazen invented the sand wedge by putting a flange on a niblick, making sand shots much easier. My father counterattacked by redesigning the eleventh and sixteenth holes, using water as the main hazard."

It's all happened before. Wood shafts gave way to steel, and golf balls evolved in distinct and dramatic stages, from feather-stuffed leather to spin-free Surlyn. Golfers evolved from Vardon to Nicklaus to Woods. Course designers and remodelers respond now as they always have—by adding length and moving bunkers. And in this Darwinian world some great courses, constricted by their property lines, cannot be made long enough to survive as championship tests. Thus it has always been. Get used to it.

"There's no way to 'Tiger-proof' a course, nor should you try," Jones says. "When I see Michael Jordan soaring above the hoop, I don't think the basket's too low. Pavorotti can hit the high C—that doesn't mean we should change the scales. Let's celebrate Tiger's genius, not waste our time trying to legislate against it."

Jones declaims interestingly on other topics, such as the Supreme Court decision ordering the PGA Tour to allow handicapped golf pro Casey Martin, once Tiger's teammate at Stanford, to ride a golf cart in competition. "What's next?" Jones asks, not sounding like a Democrat. "Will the federal government require hand rails in bunkers? Cart paths very close to greens and tees?"

Later this day, Phil Mickelson makes a hole in one on the sixth, a 174-yard shot, with an eight iron. No one remarks on the prodigious length of his short iron, just its accuracy. A generation ago, 174 meant a decision between a five iron and a six. What's next? you wonder. Will they make a ball that goes 184 with an eight iron? Or 194? Neither the Supreme Court nor the equipment manufacturers seem to give a flip about golf.

AS USUAL, Tiger tries to educate the people asking him questions. He shoots 71 in his second round, for a five-over-par total of 145, which makes the halfway cut by just one. He's had to chip and putt like a magician to do it, because his striking this week is merely good, and the golf course is so hard, and so long. Bluntly and between the lines, Woods reminds the inmates in the media tent of some simple truths: Golf is too random and the golf swing is too human and intricate for him to be the best every single time he tees it up. He is not a machine. The inanimate golf ball doesn't know who is hitting it. U.S. Open courses are very difficult. Stuff happens, but he will never feel too sorry for himself, or become too aware of the other guys, and he will never, never give up.

"I'm trying as hard as I can, but sometimes things don't go your way," Woods says. "And there's nothing you can do about it, just go out and try as hard as you can. . . . That's just the way it is sometimes." He sits on an upholstered chair on a green-carpeted platform in front of a USGA logo in a big room off the bigger main room. He's the judge in this courtroom and the reporters sitting on beige metal folding chairs and leaning forward to try to catch every nuance are a very large jury in golf clothes. To the right of the stage, transcriptionist Teresa Rider of ASAP Sports touches the silent keys on her Stentura 2000, a phonetic, syllabic typewriter. "Most people speak between 180 to 200 words per minute," says Renee Harris, Ms. Rider's writing partner. "Tiger's a 190. And he usually uses complete sentences, which is great."

Someone asks His Honor about his technique. Tiger has been trying to hit an occasional hook, a right-to-left curveball that's helpful on the fifth, seventh, and twelfth holes. But he can't quite pull it off. "I'm trying to hit a high sweeper, and I'm trying to get the club down in front of me. I'm releasing a little early to try to get the club down in front and close a little early before impact, try to get the toe of the club kind of releasing early, and, unfortunately, I'm lowering my body a little bit, too, and I hit it fat.

"I'm trying one shot at a time. That's all I can do. I can't control what the cut is going to be, all I can control is my own shots and that's all I focused on all day long today."

Twice more he speaks of his intention to hit one shot at a time, possibly the worst cliché in sports. What the hell else Tiger, the cynic mutters, two shots at a time, or three? He could have used the current sports psychologists' mantra—"staying in the present"—an equally annoying phrase that means about the same thing. But however it's expressed, "one shot at a time" is actually a profound and difficult goal. Fear bleeds into the mind of the lesser performer, whose memory of negative results is photographic. Tiger's ability to attach his mind to single swings—without worry or regret—is one of his greatest strengths.

A final question, mysteriously phrased: What gives you the logic to keep the confidence to win the championship?

"It's a U.S. Open, and if you can play a good, solid round you can get yourself up the leader board," Tiger replies. "For example, what Brooks is doing out there." As the TV monitors and scoreboards in the Media Center remind everyone, Mark David Brooks is busy burning up the place. The PGA champion of 1996 has birdied five of the first six holes. Who does he think he is, Hogan?

Yes. A couple of his peers tell you exactly that, that Brooks identifies explicitly with the original hard case from Texas. Although he's hardly the self-deluding type, he does share a number of attributes with the late Ben Hogan—hometown (Fort Worth), cigarettes, intensity, physical size, confidence, and a tendency to be abrupt with the media. The late-blooming Hogan won U.S. Opens when he was thirty-seven, thirty-eight, and forty. Brooks is forty. For a long time, including his glory year of 1996, he played Hogan equipment, had the big script *Hogan* on his golf bag. Then Callaway made a convincing argument for this rising star to change to its equipment, and he did, but his game went into a tailspin. What Would Hogan Do? Brooks walked away from his Callaway and its check for about one million a year.

Now playing Cleveland clubs, Brooks shoots 64 in the company of John L. Lewis, who is also from Texas, also forty, and also tied for the lead at the end of the day at four under with Goosen. J.L. and Mark are old friends and they have a very happy day together.

Fewer smiles erupt in the Dennis gallery, as Clark shoots 77 to miss the cut by ten. The tall, dark-haired Bamberger walks and talks for a while with Daisy, Clark's blonde, myopic mother, who doesn't like what she can't see. She kvetches and he nods sympathetically, scribbling shorthand in a little notebook. Vicki, Clark's wife, stays optimistic about a potential late rally even as the evidence mounts that it's just not in him today. Others in the Dennis posse trudge along, trying to look suitably morose as the bogies pile up like old newspapers. But they make whispered plans for dinner, and for drinks next door to Tiger.

A similar but not identical somberness hangs over the Howell-Nicklaus-Smith party. Birdies are too few and too late to matter, as all three players miss the cut, Howell by three and the others by six. But the close friends and family of Charles and Heather are too giddy about next week's trip to Hawaii for the wedding to mope over his 75-74. Meanwhile Jack and Barbara walk briskly along the yellow nylon ropes. The crowd on the perimeter of most fairways is one deep, but those watching Jack watching Gary create a moving bulge of humanity, an effect like a snake swallowing a mouse.

The group that gathers at Bob and Kim's that night is calmer than the time before. No one addresses rude comments or marriage proposals to Tiger in his twenty-thousand-dollar-a-week house beyond the tall trees, and no one jumps clothed into the pool. Tulsa's lights below are diffused and soft and the stars above are hard pinpricks. From the top deck, the wine and the night and the height lead to long reflective looks into the dark distance. The golf instructor worries about all the lessons he's got to give back in Dallas this weekend and wonders if Clark Dennis should be taking one of them. What would he emphasize, what would he say to help him get his game back? The lawyer thinks about putting his practice on hold for three or four weeks and caddying for Clark in Australia this winter. The writer compares himself to the double voyeurs observing Nicklaus observing. He recalls standing close to Tiger on practice tees and in media centers, giving him books, writing him notes, reading everything about him, even *The Soul of Tiger Woods*, and now, barely resisting the impulse to walk next door and ring his doorbell. And he remembers thinking about interviewing the girl who sold him a pack of gum the day before yesterday. Was it the Dubbl Bubbl, after all?

There is no dignity in this approach, he decides, and little insight in minutiae. Evaluating Tiger's varied impact this way is like studying a great painting with the nose three inches from the canvas. Maybe it's time to pull back.

"HE HAS THAT AURA about him where you're really intimidated," says Jeff Quinney. The twenty-two-year-old U.S. Amateur champion had been paired with Tiger for the first two rounds, and inquiring minds want to know what it was like. "I think even the top guys in the world would admit they're a little intimidated." Quinney's awe results in scores of 82-73, but Tiger removes some of the sting with a short consolation speech. "I know you didn't finish the way you wanted to," he says to the younger man, "but you really handled yourself well and I'm proud of you for that." Tiger's sportsmanlike gesture is very like the ones Nicklaus always made.

And his refusal to say he is out of it when he really is out of it—nine shots behind with eighteen to play—also sounds like Jack back in the day. Tiger shoots 69 on Saturday, but Goosen, Brooks, Mickelson, Stewart Cink, and Mediate have left him in the dust. No they haven't, Tiger says. "Anybody that's within ten can still win the tournament," Woods says. "Paul Lawrie proved that at the 1999 British Open. He came from ten back to win." He really seems to believe it. He's started to hit the ball better compared to what he started the week with, but it's plain he doesn't have his usual control.

"I don't see him hitting any little draw shots, punches, cut shots on purpose," says Johnny Miller, commentating for NBC TV. "And he has every one of those shots in his repertoire. All he's doing is going with the full one, and it's either going where he wants it or it's going right a lot." Exactly.

TV concedes a Woods defeat just as reluctantly, showing virtually every shot hit by the man who ends the day in twenty-seventh place. "There has never been a golf championship—I can't even remember a sporting event—where the single focus was so much on one man," says Dan Hicks, Miller's broadcast partner on NBC. "It's been mind boggling, the microscope, even for Tiger Woods." Again, exactly right.

The cameras remain on Earl and Tida's son on Sunday. Tiger's 69 gets him a tie for twelfth, damn good considering the way he played and the scores he made the first two days. Except for providing focus for the media and the fans and the autograph people and his next-door neighbors, Woods has had little impact on the outcome. No one got the opportunity to come unglued because Tiger was breathing down his neck, because he was never in contention. He finishes seven shots out of the Monday playoff for first, caused by a comedy of putting errors on the last hole by three not-ready-for-prime-time players, Goosen, Brooks, and Cink. All three three-putt, for an inglorious finish with no celebration and no winner. Not like Tiger at all.

On Monday, the elegant and phlegmatic Goose with an N wins the U.S. Open over Brooks.

Except for Retief and Mark, all the participants have scattered. Howell heads for Hawaii and holy matrimony. The amateurs and club pros go home. Somewhere in the rural heart of Oklahoma, Strimple stops at the A-1 Git-N-Scram for a chili dog and a Coke to keep up his strength for his five-hour drive back to Dallas. As always, he stays alert for potentially great golf holes in the countryside, just as some people see patterns in the stars or faces in clouds. Most of the pros—including Tiger—head east for the next tournament, the Buick Classic in Rye, New York.

It had been a strange week, with each disjointed day of the competition bleeding into the next. Pundits pondering the Meaning of It All noted that the 2001 U.S. Open marked the temporary end of Tiger's stranglehold on golf's major tournaments. Did this imply that his opposition was catching up? No, no one seemed to think so—Tiger finishing twelfth and the three leaders all three-putting the final green indicated only that the game is just too slippery a proposition for anyone to really control it. Southern Hills taught us less about Woods and more about golf.

On the other hand, there was this food for thought for his fellow competitors as they left Tulsa: Even on an off week, Tiger was better than all but eleven of them.

5

A BOWL OF LIFE

Every director bites the hand that lays the golden egg.

—Samuel Goldwyn

The sun shines bright on the gray marble and limestone buildings in downtown Cleveland. But a cool breeze off Lake Erie reminds you to keep your coat on, for it's only May 1, too soon to be thinking about tanning your arms in northeastern Ohio.

Cleveland looks prosperous and cheerful these days, in part because the steel mills have shut down and the air is much better. The water, too—not only can you catch a walleye in the big lake, you can eat it. New arenas for the local sports teams dot the inner city, adding to the upbeat feeling in the old city. There's a big oval for the Browns, a charming throwback stadium for the Indians, and the handsome concrete and steel Gund Arena, home of the

NBA's Cavs. Out on the waterfront sits a playful architectural oddity, the big glass pyramid of the Rock 'n' Roll Hall of Fame. But the most important building in town for the visiting rock stars and point guards—and for Tiger Woods—resides rather blandly at 1360 East Ninth Street, across the street from a small mall and down the block from a parking garage. It is the command and control center for a lot of modern sport and sportsmen. It is the place the money comes from. It is IMG.

In a backhand salute to its size, its power, and its hardball style, some sports agents refer to International Management Group as the Evil Empire. Others aren't so nice. If the companies that represent athletes were baseball teams, IMG would be the New York Yankees—confident to the point of arrogance, and consistently, infuriatingly successful. But even if IMG did not exist, jealousy would flavor the sports-marketing industry and so would most of the other deadly sins. Mistrust shoots out in all directions. The superstars and superstars-to-be don't think their agents are doing enough, or they're doing the wrong thing, or they're not getting a good enough price, or the 20 percent commissions they charge are too high. For their part, agents are frequently amazed at the something-for-nothing attitudes of their clients, their disloyalty, their occasional dishonesty, and their fuzzy understanding of the basic tenet of the business world—that is, to make money and keep it. Despite it all, thousand-dollar bills drop on everyone's head like leaves in the fall, because the right jock matched with the right product can sell about anything.

There'd been promoters acting as agents earlier in the

century. Most notable was Fred Corcoran, a smiling, round-faced Irishman who got a little cash and a lot of free cigarettes for Sam Snead to pitch Viceroys and Lucky Strikes, even though Snead did not smoke. (Fred did.) But the current setup didn't exist until Mark H. McCormack invented it in November 1958. McCormack was a young lawyer and a former college golfer a few years out of Duke working in Cleveland for the mellifluous-sounding firm of Arter, Hadden, Wykoff, and Van Duzer. But his ambition and wit would not permit a ten-year slog to make partner. He had an idea: Get a couple of the top golf pros under contract and book them for exhibitions at the highest prices the market would bear. Although some of the top players at the time received a pittance from companies like Spalding, Wilson, and MacGregor for playing their equipment, virtually their only other nontournament revenue stream was the exhibition, usually eighteen holes on a Monday in a town so out of the way it could never hope to host a full tournament.

"Few of the pros had a representative of any kind," McCormack recalled. He and his partner Dick Taylor "were confident that golf was going to get bigger and bigger and that the pros needed a representative." Furthermore, the forceful young lawyer knew two of the top performers of 1958 well enough from college golf so that they would take a meeting—Dow Finsterwald, the former Ohio University Bobcat, and Arnold Palmer, once a Wake Forest Demon Deacon. Dow and Arnie liked what they heard from McCormack and Taylor, and thus was born National Sports Management. A year later, Palmer was so pleased with the way things had gone—McCormack was getting him as much as five hundred dollars per exhibition—that at the end of 1959 Arnie asked Mark to be his sole representative in all his business matters. "I shook hands with Arnold Palmer," McCormack recalled. " 'It's a deal,' I said. The handshake is the only contract we ever had, or ever needed." (Rest assured, however, that the hundreds of deals the two have put together over the years have been put in writing.) And thus was born IMG.

McCormack's original idea got bigger, much bigger. Through good timing and even better business instinct, he and the lawyers and marketers he hired turned his company into possibly the most powerful entity in sports. IMG attracted the best clients and found ingenious and possibly fiendish new ways to drag commissions. Some IMG-created scenarios are simply hard to grasp—like the fact that airplanes have to add fuel to their tanks for long trips, and have to add fuel to compensate for the weight of the extra fuel, and need more fuel to compensate for the compensation and on and on until you want to scream. A similarly mind-boggling situation has the writer of a book agented by IMG Literary and printed and distributed by IMG Publishing interviewing golfers who are IMG clients at an IMG-created golf tournament for which they receive appearance fees from the tournament organizer—IMG. The agency also earns fees from the sponsors, and sells the television rights, and God knows what else. It all results in a giant whirlpool of money back at 1360 East Ninth Street in Cleveland.

* * *

ALASTAIR J. JOHNSTON, Arnie's personal agent for the last thirty years, sits in a corner office on the thirteenth floor of IMG's fourteen-story building. He's also the head of IMG's worldwide golf operations; one of his underlings, Mark Steinberg, Tiger's agent, resides in a lesser office next door.

Johnston's desk sits in the middle of the room, so that his back is to his two floor-to-ceiling windows. A visitor looking over his shoulder sees a square of blue sky and the rainbow in the sunlit mist hovering above Lake Erie, just a hint of the agent's Olympian view. Based in large part on his authoritative book *The Chronicles of Golf 1457-1857,* Johnston is considered golf's most insightful and thorough historian. Behind you is a table piled high with copies of his new book, *Vardon to Woods: A Pictorial History of Golfers in Advertising.* Certainly you may have one, Johnston says. Just leave thirty dollars. His "certainly" sounds like "sairtinly"—he's Scottish. An unfairly handsome man with great teeth and a full head of wavy hair, Johnston owns homes in Pepper Pike, one of Cleveland's best suburbs, and at Isleworth, down the street from Tiger, and around the corner from McCormack. He's as rich as a Rockefeller, in other words.

A table against another wall overflows with Arnold Palmer advertising kitsch—statues and running shoes, among other things, and a magazine ad in which he professes to "stay in the swing of life" with Green Magma concentrated barley juice powder. The table serves as a reminder, Johnston says, "that licensed products must be very carefully controlled, or else they will devolve into a trash element."

Johnston impresses immediately as a well-spoken man with an instinct for the heart of the matter. For example, in *Vardon to Woods* he discusses the difficult situation of the athlete's inevitable decline. How to keep him current as an endorser of products? "It was recognized that one day Palmer would no longer win tournaments on a regular basis, and there should not be a perception in the marketplace that his value had been compromised from his disappearance from the victor's podium," Johnston writes. "The most effective image that was determined for Arnold Palmer . . . should be that of being 'successful.' " Success, Johnston points out, is more likely for most of us to achieve than winning something or other, and thus it's a goal we can relate to and strive for ourselves. This insightful marketing deepened our already strong admiration for Arnie, the best-loved American sportsman ever.

Will Tiger ever soar to his heights as a pitchman?

Johnston goes along with the inevitable but inevitably difficult Palmer-Woods comparison for a minute of two. "Yes, they're analogous in that both took golf to a new demographic," Johnston argues. "Arnold took it outside the country club and to Europe. Tiger's appeal is to an age group and an ethnic group. He's taken golf 'low,' that is, to ethnic minorities. He's made the game cooler to them."

Johnston distills a semester or two of college marketing classes in twenty minutes. He's given you the perfect example of positioning—nudging Palmer's image from tournament winner to a model of success in business and in life—and now he moves on to another big subject, branding. In football terms, the brand is the player and his positioning is where on the field he plays. "The brand evolves, and then we mold it," Johnston says. "Candidly, the brand idea is how we extract value."

And Palmer's brand is? "The quintessential American hero," Johnston says. "In Asia, especially, he's viewed as another John Wayne. Hardworking, compassionate, looks you in the eye, a charger. When filming a commercial, he always rejects the scripts he's given—he just speaks in his own idiom. People see him in one of his ads and think, 'There's a guy doing pretty well. *I'm* doing pretty well.' "

But Tiger Brand, Johnston says, "can't be compared to Arnold's. Tiger comes from a generation that does not expect to work for thirty years for recognition. A very impatient culture—they want accomplishment and riches now. Tiger is the flagship for that culture—he wants to beat all of Arnold Palmer's and Jack Nicklaus's records, and he wants to do it in five years. Tiger's is the new American face."

As the ads reproduced in Johnston's book attest, Arnie and IMG employed a shotgun approach back in the day when a good deal wasn't worth a hell of a lot. For instance, one of Palmer's earliest endorsements, for Heinz ketchup, paid just five hundred dollars. Among scores of other things, Arnie also encouraged the world to buy certain types of sunglasses, tuxedoes, lawn mowers, power tools, fire sprinklers, jets, luggage, and electron television tubes. And don't forget to pick up some Swing aftershave—"a new kind of all-man, all-day aftershave. Bold and brisk. Lots of authority. But never perfumey." And remember to drink a nice tall glass of Green Magma.

Tiger's endorsement deals are far fewer and at $10 million or so each, far more profitable. It's no great secret that Palmer resents a little bit Woods's comparatively easy path to riches and his cavalier attitude about how he attained it. After all, Arnie blazed the trail that Tiger now walks. Yes, Palmer made very good endorsement income and was the first to do so, but he wanted real wealth, not just great wages. In one of his biggest gambits, Arnold Palmer lent his name to a string of Cadillac dealerships. Not a manageable five or six but over twenty of them, eventually, in Pennsylvania and the Southeast. They didn't do well, and the manager of the group was sued several times for defaulting on loans and using money for personal expenses. An $11 million judgment obtained by Arnold Palmer and his sports agency remains unpaid. In another of his big plays, he organized the construction and financing of a housing, hotel, and golf course community in Orlando called Bay Hill. It, too, ran into huge trouble and Palmer lost millions. Like most big-time players at capitalism, in other words, Arnie has made and lost fortunes. His income continues to be enormous because he continues to work, but the idea that he has a golden touch is a myth. The details are different, of course, but Jack Nicklaus has had a long series of business ups and downs very similar to Palmer's. And he's still working, too.

Meanwhile, Tiger risks nothing but a smile. He doesn't invest a dime in American Express, Nike, Wheaties, Disney, Buick, Titleist/Footjoy, Upper Deck, or EA Sports. And why should he? Just by cashing his endorsement checks, at twenty-five he's as wealthy as or wealthier than Arnie. IMG puts it out that Tiger's superinvolved with these companies, that they are partnerships, really. This is mere spin. "They get more than just his name," wrote Ross Nethery in a Valentine to Tiger in *American Way* entitled "Six Billion Dollar Man." "They get his ideas and his intelligence. They get his energy. They get his loyalty. They get his will to win, at everything and at all costs. They get his image." But they don't get the deep concern of a man risking his own money in the big-business poker game.

"People are looking at Arnold Palmer and Tiger as the bookends of golf," Johnston says emphatically, as if his guest is missing an important and obvious point. "Sometimes we expect Tiger to act like Arnold—*but they're forty-eight years apart.* I think for a twenty-five-year-old he's doing a hell of a good job. He was trained for it, of course."

How Woods and IMG got together is another example of IMG's business brilliance. Borrowing a page from the college basketball recruiters who hire the father as an assistant coach as a way to get his coveted kid to come to State U—it's happened a couple of times—IMG employed Earl Woods as a "junior golf scout." Earl's scouting report surprised no one: Get Tiger.

Although the papers had not been signed, a deal was in place between Tiger and Nike—with IMG in the middle—when Woods played in his final event before turning pro. This was the 1996 U.S. Amateur at Pumpkin Ridge in Portland, just a fifteen- or twenty-minute drive from Nike's headquarters in Beaverton. Nike CEO Phil Knight watched Tiger win his third consecutive Amateur with undisguised delight. "Requests [from Nike] for him to shoot television commercials on the Monday after the Championship were denied on the grounds that no one would believe that such a commitment was made at short notice," writes agent Johnston carefully. "And the perceived preplanning might have prejudiced Tiger's professed amateur status." The planning wasn't only "perceived," of course, it was actual. Nike would be paying the twenty-year-old $40 million, not the kind of deal that can be consummated between the trophy presentation and dinner.

The campaign concocted by Nike and its ad agency caused a mighty stir, which is what ad campaigns are supposed to do, but for some people it created a powerful and lingering distaste for Woods and Team Tiger (meaning the player himself, his father, Nike, and IMG). The first Tiger-Nike ad appeared in the August 29, 1996, *Wall Street Journal*. Next to a large photo of a prekindergarten Tiger swinging a club at a ball, and beneath six repetitions of the phrase "Hello world," were nine separate bragging points. "I shot in the 60s when I was twelve. I played in the British Open when I was nineteen," and so on. Two final statements caused the stir: "There are still courses in the United States that I'm not allowed to play because of the color of my skin," and, "I've heard I'm not ready for you. Are you ready for me?"

Then, in his first words at his first press conference as a professional, and without irony, he said the line: "Hello world." Well—all the hellos seemed a bit stupid, since we'd already been introduced, countless times in fact, to the most exciting golfer since Arnie. As for the "world," that would have seemed like a good word to use for a company wanting to emphasize its global capabilities. That's fair enough. But the brag lines pinged the cockiness radar and annoyed the thousands of troops still loyal to humble heroes like Nicklaus, Palmer, Hogan, Nelson, and Jones. And the color issue struck many as completely bogus and offensive, a canard, a race card played to build sympathy for an athlete who was already the favorite of millions, a young man who would soon protest that everyone else talked too much about his racial makeup. Moreover, no one believed it—a golf course that would not allow the three-time Amateur champion to play? Just show us. We'll get *The Washington Post*, the FBI, and a *60 Minutes* crew out there pronto, then we'll burn the place down.

The penultimate line inspired the most columns and comment, but the final sentence—"Are you ready for me?"—provided the final clue that Nike and its ad agency did not know what they were doing. Nike had never done golf before and it clearly did not understand its audience. They'd been making their money on fancy rubber and leather shoes for basketball players, with Michael Jordan as its spokesman and gyms and urban playgrounds his stage. "You ready for me?" is trash talk, common on the asphalt in a pick-up game, but rare on the first tee. In fact, one of the things golfers like best about their game is its absence of ritual threats and leg-lifting from circling Alpha dogs, and all the chest pounding and swaggering that infect professional basketball and football. We appreciated that about Tiger, too. Or we thought we did, until he got in our face with this ad, which had the unintended effect of alienating people who wanted to like him. They could have communicated the joy Tiger feels when he plays golf, or his excitement at the prospect of competing against the best in golf while wearing quality Nike clothing, or a score of other positive messages. Instead they give us, "You ready for me?"

It's possible to put too fine a point on this, of course. Did we really think that was Sam Snead talking in his 1950s testimonials for car tires? "Look inside a B.F. Goodrich tire," the smiling cartoon head of Slammin' Sam said. "You'll see the cords have no cross threads—they're free to flex in rhythm to give you Rhythm Ride—with more miles, safety, and comfort!" But we accepted the copy in the Nike ad as Tiger's own words because IMG-Nike-Woods seemed like a monolith with one voice.

At any rate, the "You ready for me?" ads were quickly replaced with the "I Am Tiger Woods" series. This second curious tag line was almost laughably manipulative. Delivered by a black kid, a white one, an Asian one, a Hispanic one, another black, another white, and so on—it told us in so many words that we identify with uni-racial Tiger, and we identify so deeply we "are" him. But identification is slow and personal and doesn't occur because a giant advertiser says it has, and the Rainbow Coalition thing felt like more force-feeding.

But the most valuable Tiger commercial is the one that never stops. Tiger keeps his swoosh visible at all times, so we never get one without the other. He wears the hat with the fat check mark during tournament rounds (of course) and in trophy presentations, interviews, even in his ads for other products. With a new five-year deal worth $100 million in place, his Nike-Nike-Nike-Nike will continue.

But there's danger in Tiger's cloth tattoo. Some people are getting sick of it. Its annoying ubiquity caused a participant in a recent athletic shoe focus group to refer to the logo as a "swooshstika." By believing too fervently in the value of repeated exposure, and by doing its job too well, the swoosh is devolving into the infuriating smiley faces of a few years ago, which we tuned out, then, thank you Jesus, stamped out. Nike addresses the oversaturation problem with sublogos, such as the jumping-man symbol for Michael Jordan and a new stylized TW for Tiger. That might not be enough. Maybe it's time for a makeover, a new corporate symbol and a new name.

It should be pointed out that Nike manufactures nothing or almost nothing: An army of subcontractors around the world actually makes its products. Its golf ball, for instance, is currently built and swooshed by Bridgestone of Japan, Wilson of the United States, and two factories in China. By keeping itself free to concentrate on designing and selling its stuff, Nike became a marketing master, and a quick study in what works and what doesn't. After the tedious political posturing of its first campaigns, the company delivered two commercials that worked pretty well. In the first, ad-libbed—and performed perfectly on just the fifth take—Tiger bounces a ball off the face of his sand wedge this way and that, then caroms the ball up high a final time, swings like a baseball player, and whacks it out of sight. In the second commercial, a rangeful of hackers starts hitting perfect shots in unison with Tiger and we hear a

Viennese waltz. Then Woods leaves the practice tee, the music stops, and the practicing golfers revert to their bad old ways. Although traditionalists might wish to see *something* about the product, the message in these spots is probably the right one: Tiger is amazing.

"The big deal these days is brand relevancy," comments Pat Madden, a five-handicap golfer and the owner of an ad agency in San Francisco. "Every brand develops a more or less formal description of its personality. Nike and the others are trying to say that their brand is relevant to Tiger's, that they overlap in some way or complement each other. When the two brands line up, the endorsement works. When they don't, you've got a commercial nothing can save."

Wheaties achieves brand relevance by delivering a simple message simply: Tiger is a hero, in the same league as other Wheaties Champions whose image has graced their orange box of dry brown cereal since the 1930s. American Express's print ads passed the test, but its TV commercials were hip and incomprehensible. In one, Tiger plays golf through an inner city and onto or into his target, a spot between the railroad tracks on an elevated bridge. The tortured point being that Tiger is prepared for anything, even city buses and skyscrapers between him and his goal, and you will be, too, with the American Express card. "You can always tell when the [ad agency] art director isn't a golfer," Madden says. Higher marks go to Buick, whose ads oxygenated Tiger Brand with a bit of humor. In one spot, he poked fun at himself by having his "students," identically clad in his black and red Sunday uniform, practice his trademark fist pump, and his infamous statement after winning that "I didn't have my 'A' game." Then they all drive off in identical four-door black Buicks. But Tiger in a Buick leaves an uneasy, discordant feeling. We know he's making more than $50 million a year—why would he drive such a humble vehicle? The answer: When money talks, brand relevance walks.

THE VICE PRESIDENT of Corporate Communications for each of the companies that Tiger endorses will tell you that they're thrilled with their association with Mr. Woods and that their stockholders are too. There's no reason not to believe Kirk Stewart of Nike or Judy Tenzer of American Express or Pete Ternes of Buick, except that their jobs and their perspectives compel them to sing a happy song. But is Nike's $20 million a year, Amex's annual $5 million, and the big bucks from Buick money well spent? Nike stock sold for fifty-five dollars a share in August 1996, when it signed Tiger, spiked to seventy-three dollars in March '97 when Tigermania peaked, then slowly slid into a slough of thirty-five dollars a share in 2001. Tracking stock prices is a completely unfair way to judge an endorser's impact, however. As big as Tiger is, he's like a gnat on an elephant's behind compared to global market forces.

Measuring his business impact is tricky: Straightforward golf gives you a score at the end of the day but big business leaves you guessing. You've got sales volume and stock price and overhead but how much did your advertising affect the numbers? Measuring effectiveness is the essence of the advertising problem. Judging the impact of the pitchman within a campaign—Tiger—may be impossible. In a famous study, a professor at the Wharton School at the University of Pennsylvania, and a member of the board of directors of beer-maker Anhaeuser Busch, was commissioned by the brewery to perform a multivariable analysis of the factors affecting its sales. Professor Russ Ackoff considered everything he could under the general categories of price, product, place, and promotion, including the effects of celebrity endorsers. His conclusion: The only thing that stimulates beer sales is warm weather.

So why would a corporation annually spend a king's ransom on a twenty-five-year-old whose time is stretched so tightly it's about to snap, a young man who is not about to have drinks and tell stories to your ten best customers? Well, corporate decision-making is not a science. Received wisdom tells the corporation it's got to spend some of its millions on advertising—because its competitors do and surely will in the future. Perhaps the decision-makers want a big name to keep the other guys in the industry from getting him. Maybe the company hires a golfer because the chairman plays golf, and everyone's life is a little easier if the boss is happy. In Nike's case, its huge corporate ego virtually demands hiring the endorsement of the biggest star in each of its sporting goods fields: Michael Jordan in basketball, Michael Johnson in track, Mia Hamm in women's soccer, Woods in golf. The company dominates equipment sales in the first three sports and aims to swallow up golf as well. So help them Tiger.

Since there's no certain cause and effect between the

celebrity endorsement and the consumer getting out his credit card, judging Tiger's effectiveness comes down to educated guesses and anecdotes. Independent Nike representative Jim Quinn provides both at the merchandise tent on Wednesday of Open week at Southern Hills. But if you want to talk, you're going to have to do what he's doing, which is carry box after box of Nike golf balls with U.S. Open logos from storage to the display shelf. With his fifth consecutive win in a major still a possibility, everyone wants Tiger's balls. People snatch them up by the sleeve or by the dozen almost as fast as Quinn puts them out. "We've only got one more carton of these left," he says. He says that a few times.

"Golf is Nike's smallest but fastest-growing division," says Quinn, a bespectacled forty-five-year-old father of six in the middle of a fourteen-hour day. "Everything is so far up, it's crazy. Apparel's up 70 percent over last year. Balls, 700 percent. Shoes, 90 percent. Bags 400 percent."

Quinn pauses at the Nike shirt rack after another trip to the storage area on the perimeter of the tent. The shirts cost sixty-five to eighty dollars each. "Unit sales of shirts have increased from 35,000 to 350,000. The three biggest in volume are Ashworth, Cutter and Buck, and Polo. Nike could catch and pass at least one of them next year, if they can get the quality up."

While Quinn shows off the new "TW" logo making its debut this week, he's reminded that some pros at high-end clubs—Tad Weeks at Champions in Houston, for example—don't stock a single thread of Nike. "There were some initial quality, shipping, and style issues," he says. "We were more athletic at first, and the shirts looked like they were for basketball. The wrong stuff by the wrong designers. Golfers are thirty to fifty, not twenty. But now the shirts are being designed in Italy.

"How much of the success can be credited to Tiger? With the ball, almost all of it. After he won the U.S. and British Opens last year, the people I was calling on began to say, 'You've really got something here,' and they began to buy. But the truth is, Titleist has kicked everyone's ass in the premium golf ball market with their Pro V1. As for apparel, it's a combination of better design and the fact that Tiger's wearing it. Golf bags and shoes—he's had no impact on that."

While Nike golf products dovetail with what Tiger does for a living and its youthful and aggressive marketing meshes with his style, Buick seems like a stretch. The Buick division of General Motors makes comfortable cars for a conservative, mature market segment but Woods, if he were a car, would be something with a lot of horsepower and great lines, a Ferrari or a Lamborghini. "Which is exactly the point," says Mark McCormack, leaving his questioner to fill in the obvious blanks. Oh, gotcha. Buick hopes proximity to Tiger will rub some jazz on its stodgy reputation.

This may be good for the car company, but is it good for Tiger? After Fuzzy Zoeller and Chip Beck went down-market by pitching for Kmart and Wal-Mart, they said permanent goodbyes to upscale endorsements. You can move down the food chain, marketers say—from Neiman Marcus to Sears, for example—but you can't go up. Tiger should be a Cadillac, at least, but he's a Buick. Specifically, a Rendezvous, which is now the name painted on his golf bag. He started as a Regal.

"He's given us a whole new level of visibility," says Buick product specialist Joni Wilson. "He's the ultimate representative. He breaks down all barriers between himself and older white men." Ms. Wilson is glib and gorgeous and she's happy to give you a thorough tour of the white Rendezvous on display under an awning connected to a trailer behind the clubhouse at the Texas Open in San Antonio. She mentions the four hundred thousand "dealer commitments" for the Rendezvous, which purports to be a combination of minivan, SUV, and passenger car. This one's got the CX Luxury Package, which includes leather seats, a sunroof, and an emergency system called On Star. It gets nineteen miles per gallon city, twenty-six on the highway. The final cost of a new loaded 'Vous is $31,585, which may not be so downmarket after all.

"I met him," Wilson says. "He talked to me. It was in the buffet line at the Buick Classic at Westchester, during one of the many rain delays. He said, 'How are you today?' I asked him about his score. He said, 'It's not too good—don't remind me.'" Tiger was in the midst of shooting 75 in his first round after the U.S. Open, his highest score of the year. He shot 66 the next day.

"I think it's admirable that he's endorsing cars the average person can afford," Wilson says, food for thought for those who embrace the brand relevancy idea. "He's a gentleman. And he's every man's hero."

Joni Wilson, Jim Quinn, Phil Knight, Mark McCormack, a thousand employees at Buick, a million customers of Nike . . . Tiger's impact on the business world is both immeasurable and monumental. And interesting, too, when his endorsements bump and compete. For instance, Woods played in the MasterCard Colonial in 1997, was embraced like a prodigal son by the fans in Fort Worth, and finished tied for fourth. But he's never gone back, and instead flies to Dusseldorf for the Deutsche Bank German Open, an IMG event (surprise) for which he gets a $2.5-million appearance fee (such payments are not permitted on the PGA Tour). The people at the MasterCard Colonial suspect that the lure is not the money or the strudel but that American Express doesn't want him in a competing credit card company's tournament.

A similar skirmish of corporate titans took place early in the year. Tiger won the first event of 2000, the Mercedes Championships, and the promotional material for the 2001 tournament naturally featured the image of the defending champ. Woods squawked about this, fearing, apparently, that anyone might think he'd forsaken his Rendezvous and its nineteen city, twenty-six highway, and was now standing behind the Benz.

Tiger's golf club deals with Nike and Titleist conflict in a particularly complicated way, an inevitable state of affairs for two reasons. First, these two competitors battle like Arabs and Jews anyway. Second, golf club endorsement is often so misleading that disagreements simply must occur. It's as if the celebrity smiled for the camera and bit into a Big Mac—only his specially equipped, prototype Big Mac has filet mignon inside instead of fried burger. "Yes, Tiger plays Titleist, and he's not gonna change," says Larry Bobka, the parent company Acushnet's senior vice president PGA/LPGA Promotions—Golf Clubs. "If I was playing as well as he is, I wouldn't change my *socks.*"

Tiger's club deal is indeed with Titleist. You can buy clubs that are identical to his driver, three wood, putter, and wedges. Titleist is stamped on his irons, too, but they're not like any Titleist clubs you can buy—they're actually very good replicas of the forged Mizuno irons he played for many years. Nike's getting into the club business, too, so it wants to replace Tiger's fake Titleists with fake Nikes. They had a set made up for him by a custom golf club grinder in Fort Worth. Tiger loved them. But Butch Harmon, his instructor, did not. No, T, he said, you can't play these. Turns out Butch is on the Titleist payroll.

But IMG wins no matter what clubs Tiger plays, as long as he stays in the fold. But some wonder if Tiger needs McCormack and company anymore. Nicklaus left in the late sixties and formed his own management company, Golden Bear, when he saw that Palmer would always be number one at IMG. Like Jack, many name brand golf pros jettison their agents in early middle age as they reach their peak years as earners and gain confidence as businessmen. Some insiders think a split is therefore inevitable; others say Tiger will stay because he is the first among equals at IMG, not Palmer and not one of IMG's big-dollar athletes from other sports, like baseball player Alex Rodriguez of the Texas Rangers. Others say he'll stay because he owns a piece of the action. There are precedents. Phil Mickelson has a percentage of his agent's television division. Charles Howell owns 5 percent of Hambric Sports Management.

To the extent that Tiger's departure would hurt IMG, certain disgruntled former clients would love to see it. "Tear them a new one," they tell a writer. "The stories I could tell . . ." But they don't reveal the shocking behind-the-scenes truth about the world's largest sports-marketing agency because they can't. Because a divorce from IMG goes something like this: The unhappy player says adios, and the agent says I'm sorry it didn't work out, we had some great years together, good luck. But by the way, you owe us three hundred thousand dollars—the present value of the multi-year deals we negotiated for you. The player tells the agent to do something impossible to himself, then wonders aloud why in hell he thinks he deserves a commission on *future* income? Each threatens to sue the other. Finally IMG lets the player out of the contract, for some percentage of the lifetime value of the endorsements. But it also gets Joe Pro's signature on a document that says he can never talk about the breakup, or about anything internal to IMG.

This doesn't seem sporting to the golfers, but the brutal truth is that as businessmen, they are 20-handicappers. They've got volumes to learn about making it and keeping it despite their association with the guys who wrote the book. And after they leave to find new representation the sun will still shine on IMG, in Cleveland by the lake, the Tiger Woods of agents.

*   *   *

BEFORE HE BEGAN doing nine years in a federal prison, someone asked Bruce McNall, the king of sports crooks, why he did it. The rotund owner of the Los Angeles Kings of the National Hockey League and chairman of the board of the NHL bilked investors and banks out of about $200 million and lived a life light-years beyond his means. Why? McNall repeated that old saw that the Brinks truck never follows the hearse to the cemetery. But when it came down to it, he said, maybe it was the jet. The expense was enormous but getting into and out of his own magic carpet was a feeling he could not live without.

It's July, and Charles Howell is talking about jets. For a while now he's known about their cost and capabilities, but he's used the knowledge only to tease John Engler. Engler's an All-American college golfer from back home in Augusta who dearly wants what Charles has, that is, a place on the PGA Tour and the riches and perquisites attendant thereto. "Oh yeah, we're taking a Citation X to Texas, but for longer trips, we really prefer the Gulfstream V," Howell would say to the wide-eyed Engler, at a time when Delta, American, and United were actually ferrying Heather and him around the country. But now jet-leasing and fractional-ownership companies are talking, and Howell is listening.

A couple of things have changed since the U.S. Open in Tulsa. He got married, of course, a weeklong, alcohol-free, golf-filled, family-only celebration in Hawaii. But Milwaukee meant more than Maui, vis-à-vis private jet transportation. After starting the Greater Milwaukee Open with 66-69-67, Howell birdied the final four holes of his Sunday round, and six of the last seven, for a 64. Two groups behind him,

Shigeki Maruyama was shooting a miraculous or flukish 66—he holed a full five-iron shot early in the round, and got away with a three wood into the grandstand on the eighteenth. But the short, stocky Japanese tied the strong, skinny American for first. Shigeki-san won the one-hole playoff, but Charles got a check for $334,800. He'd won three-quarters of a million for the year, and had, in effect, secured himself a place on the Tour for the rest of 2001 and all of 2002.

Every frequent traveler in line imagines the bliss of going right to the door of his or her own jet, with no delays for ticketing, check-in, security, or boarding, and then the crew's not ready, or the plane's not stocked with shrink-wrapped "bistro meals." Now Howell could hear the numbers for leasing or fractional ownership of a little jet without laughing or crying. "Enjoy unmatched flexibility and economy, as well as convenient access to any category of private jet," went the pitch from Executive Business Jets. "Your flight will be confirmed upon receipt of an authorized credit card." Did they say "economy"? There's a relative term—a company called Flight Options offers Howell a four-seat Citation I on call for $195,000 up front, $4,100 a month for maintenance, plus $995 per hour the plane is in the air on his behalf. But as a man with the frank goal of being the best in the world, he only has to ask WWTD? Tiger would go for it, and use the savings of time and energy for more rest and more work.

But even as Howell prepares to move into the rarefied air of the private jet set, his surroundings remind him that he isn't yet in the same sentence or the same foursome with

Woods, Mickelson, and Duval. Because until either a year passes or he wins a tournament, he is not even an official member of the PGA Tour. And he hasn't won enough money and is not highly enough ranked on the world list to receive an exemption for golf's real party the third week of July—the British Open. So instead here is Howell at the Wednesday pro-am at the B.C. Open in Endicott, New York, a town and a tournament that time forgot.

"I said to my husband, 'If I can get him, I want Charles Howell III,' " says Donna Sands. She's a first-year volunteer at the B.C.—named for the comic strip drawn by local resident Johnny Hart, not for British Columbia—and her wish to keep score for Howell and his four amateur partners has come true. She'd watched on television on Sunday as Howell almost won in Milwaukee and had been impressed with the graceful way he handled himself. "He's the kind of boy any mother would want for a son," says Mrs. Sands.

"Can I take your picture?" asks a spectator after Howell hits his drive off the fifth tee. "I hear you're gonna be famous." Howell smiles good-naturedly, more the adult in this interaction than the three-times-his-age photographer. "Charles doesn't know how good he's got it," comments caddie Ron "Bambi" Levin on the walk up the fairway. "He can still go to a mall or a restaurant. I don't think that will be possible in a year or two."

If that is true, Bambi will achieve a certain celebrity himself. The media will seek out his point of view, and there will be autograph requests, even endorsement opportunities. "I'll deflect everything," Levin says. "You see the way Steve Williams handles it. And you see what happened to

Fluff." Williams is Tiger's famously reticent caddie; Fluff Cowan, Williams's predecessor, enjoyed his reflected glory rather too much for the boss's taste, and was fired.

Both Charles and Bambi are gifted conversationalists who observe moments of silence while someone's hitting a shot. Otherwise, they're yakking. Levin will not let Howell hit a shot, even in a practice round, without first saying something. "Anything to keep him thinking," he says. "The worst thing you can do is let him step up there with no target or no thought." Howell listens to his caddie's quiet instruction—"It's 280 to the corner. Take it right over that tree"—hits his shot, hands the club back to Bambi, and resumes talking. He has pages to say about Ely Callaway, the founder of the company whose equipment he plays, who has just died. "He was an awesome man, never lacked for a new idea, and I agreed with him about making golf an easier game. He called me every three weeks just to see how I was doing." After he crushes a tee shot about 320 and straight, someone asks him why he's not playing the Pro V1, the most popular golf ball on Tour. "Because it's the worst ball on Tour. It's compression-molded, so it has a seam, and it goes farther if you hit it where the two halves come together. See, the Callaway ball is injection-molded, no seam. On the tee, everyone who plays the Pro V1 hits it on the seam, and it goes farther. The problem comes in the fairway. What am I gonna do, say, 'Bambi, it's 150, but it's on the seam, so it will play 140?' "

A new edict from the USGA allowing kids as young as seventeen to attempt to qualify for the PGA Tour and retain their amateur status if they do not make it also floats

Howell's boat. "You're gonna have a seventeen-year-old qualify, then come out here and get his brains beat in for a year, " he says. "Then what? I don't think they thought that one through."

Someone asks Howell why the grip on his putter is transparent. "Well, it felt good when I tried it," he says. "Plus, I love being different." Perhaps because he only recently matriculated at Oklahoma State, he observes the culture of the Tour with an academic's dispassion. "I guarantee 90 percent of our players are from a wealthy background. Everyone dresses alike and swings similar. I had this talk with Jesper Parnevik. In the NBA, Dennis Rodman had to try really hard to be different. All Jesper does is flip up his hat brim and he's got an identity. Arnold Palmer hasn't won since '73 but he's still doing commercials, why, because he has an identity. In the grand scheme of things, we're simply entertainers. And our window in terms of marketing ourselves is very small."

As for his own identity, Howell has plans. When the offers get right, and like the other players he wants to stand apart from, he will become a human billboard. A watch company logo on the bag, a luxury car sign on the left chest and left collar, an investment company on the left sleeve, and the shirtmaker's own insignia on the right sleeve and over the shoulder blades. "I want to be affiliated with well-known and well-liked companies," he says. "Since my main endorsement is with Callaway, they have to approve. So you're not gonna see me wearing a Trojans Condoms logo."

The five golfers and five caddies continue their march.

On a par 5 hole on the second nine, Bambi says "Here comes the devil."

Ted Tryba walks through the trees bordering a parallel fairway. An eight-year Tour veteran with the physique and good looks of a B movie leading man, Tryba (TREE-buh), wants to congratulate Charles on his near win at Milwaukee. In a similar conference a few months before, Ted, thirty-four, a connoisseur of the single life, had told Howell that getting married could be a grave mistake. "What if we're at the Los Angeles Open, and we get invited to the Playboy mansion?" he asked rhetorically. The younger man just laughed, and asked Tryba if he would ever walk down the aisle. "Only if I lose my mojo," he replied.

On the pro golf tour, everybody does something about sex but nobody talks about it. With the demise of the pro-am cocktail party and the dramatic rise in the money at stake, it's a far more chaste environment than it used to be. The best stories from the eighties and earlier would easily fill a few Jackie Collins novels but—with some exceptions—today's touring pros would be as likely to get their tongues pierced as to seek romantic adventure away from home. When crowds press close on the walk from the scorer's trailer to the locker room, and knowing how much some of them want to overhear something salacious, Willie Wood sometimes tells snippets of a very hot but completely fictional encounter: "And then she tied my hands and feet to the bedposts, and then she poured a circle of gasoline around the bed. And then she struck a match and the flames were this high and she . . ."

Actual assignations still take place, of course, occasionally enabled by the big-time golf pro's mobile aphrodisiac, the courtesy car. Sometimes go-for-broke women will spot the tournament logo on the side of a pearlized white Cadillac and they'll catch the driver's eye at a light and make the roll-down-your-window gesture, although of course the fancy courtesy car has power windows. "Wanna go have a drink?" they may say. "Wanna come to a party at my apartment?" The proper response is "hell no" but accidents do happen.

No such thing occurs at the B.C. Open, however, which in terms of purse and media attention is the smallest tournament on the Tour. The courtesy cars are few and inconspicuous and they are Buicks, not Cadillacs, and the town is largely populated by eleven thousand IBM retirees, precious few of whom are crazy young women. Thomas Watson founded International Business Machines in nearby Armonk, New York, and the company still thrives here but in counterpoint to the forlorn, abandoned buildings of Endicott-Johnson, a shoe company, which went bankrupt twenty years ago. At its height, EJ employed twenty thousand local citizens. Now, it employs none.

There's something in the melancholic air of the place and the event that reminds you of the heart of professional golf, a heart that Tiger's never known and never will know: Golf's a very hard game, and the road's a lonely place.

Caddies always seem to be in touch with the golfer's blues. Bambi Levin, for example, didn't always have a bag so good he could afford to fly from tournament to tournament, as he does now (his previous employer was Gary Nicklaus). Once Bambi and three other caddies squeezed into a blue Honda Civic and drove coast to coast, from Palm Springs to Miami. A little past halfway, their car broke down in Hattiesburg, Mississippi, and the mechanic said it would take him a day to get parts. One day turned into two, and two into three. When the loopers finally got their car back, its interior was littered with baby bottles and disposable diapers, a couple of them used, plain evidence that the car hadn't really been out of commission for seventy-two hours.

In Endicott, the sad heart of the tour beats strong at the aging Econo-Lodge across West Main Street from the golf course, a one-hundred-yard walk from the front gate. A pink sunset streaks the July sky and gleams softly on the hotel's aluminum siding and the vacancy light is lit. A man of middle years in clean, worn golf clothes holds the lobby door open, because he thinks you might be a player, and he's a caddie without a job. Mike, he says, extending his hand, how are you, here for the tournament? He's been on the prowl since 4:30 this morning. His girlfriend is highly dubious about this timeline but she don't know golfers, Mike says.

"Mark Pfeil's plane arrives at 9:02, but I don't know which airport," Mike says. "I'm pretty sure he's checkin' in here at the Econo, and if he gets here and it all works out, hey, I got a job." Pfeil (pronounced "file") hasn't cashed a check on the Tour since 1998—$3,258 for a tie for fifty-eighth right here in Endicott—but he's the kind of guy who is invited to fill up the field at the B.C. Open.

As the guest checks in with hotel owner Pete Bhoola, Mike remains as close as a point guard on defense and keeps up the chatter. He gestures frequently with a pencil at a notepad that's dense with names and numbers, and 9:02 is underlined twice. Sure, Mike says, he'd like to have dinner—"All I've eaten all day is a bowl of life." Bhoola snickers at this mystical comment from the caddie who's been pacing in his lobby since sunrise. Yeah, right, a bowl of life! But Mike says he means Life breakfast cereal, a product of the Quaker Oats Company.

Next door is Russell's, an architectural match for the Econo, but with a long green canopy from the front door to the parking lot that gives it an air of occasion. Mike has the steak. A chronological storyteller, he begins the tale of his life even before his own birth. "My father was part of a test and had some atomic substance injected in his veins during World War II and he wound up on disability," he says. "Mom said he never had a normal night's sleep the rest of his life. He jumped. He didn't want me to go in the army."

Mike's dry now but his own problems with substances started when as an altar boy he repeatedly filched the sacramental wine. They gave him an extra forty days in Vietnam for drunkenness but three days of R and R "for accidentally capturing an RVN captain. So I go to this restaurant in Bangkok and they've got this drink, a pastiche [pastis] made from Pernord [Pernod] and it's opiated. Oh, man."

His job in war foreshadowed his job as a civilian: As the assistant to an M-60 man, Mike carried around a thousand rounds of 7.62-millimeter ammunition for the automatic weapon. The other guy fired the gun. "Vietnam was the tourist war," Mike says. "These CIA guys would come in wearing shorts and Hawaiian shirts. But they acted like Hapsburgs or Hohenzollerns, wouldn't even talk to you."

But he follows that bit of erudition with a stumbling, self-interrupting monologue, as he tries to recall the interlude between 1970, when he got out of the service, and the start of his career as a professional caddie in 1984. VA hospitals, liquor bottles, and post-traumatic stress syndrome seemed to have been the mile markers on that long, lonely road.

"They don't know that much about PTSD even if they say they do," Mike says. "So this was in—when? I don't know so we play in . . . I don't know. And was that before Omaha? And I go to Vegas not for a tournament but to see some friends, caddies. Did you know the Chief? Anyway, I like to play casino craps . . ."

After dinner Pfeil finally arrives and he hires Mike to carry his clubs. If the caddie really was the Taoist he seemed to be for a minute, he might say that without Pfeil and himself, Tiger Woods and his wealthy carrier Steve Williams would not exist. "Under heaven, all can see beauty as beauty only because there is ugliness," says the Tao Te Ching. "Therefore having and not having arise together. Difficult and easy complement each other. Long and short contrast each other. High and low rest on each other."

All eat from the bowl of life. Tiger just has a bigger spoon.

NOTHING MUCH HAPPENS at the B.C. Open and no one much cares. The crowds don't really deserve the name, and they are quiet, too quiet. Maybe it's the soporific effect of the gentle weather combined with the water music from the fountains spewing inside every rock- or concrete-block-lined water hazard. Perhaps it's their sheer lack of numbers that cause the sixteen fans by the third green to erupt in silence when rookie Ben Curtis sticks a full wedge eighteen inches from the hole, well inside the unofficial applause zone at other tournaments.

Players pause by TVs from time to time to watch the big show in golf. PGA Tour professional David Ogrin expresses regret that he is not playing Over There. But most pronounce themselves to be well-pleased to be here in the Tri-Cities. "I could mow a strip of grass in a hayfield and call it a fairway," says Scott Gump, a veteran of the infamous '99 British Open at Carnoustie. "And I could cut out a circle at the end and call it a green."

The biggest excitement of the week occurs at the end of the first day. "We've got a better leader board than they do," says B.C. Open tournament director Mike Norman. "They" have Colin Montgomerie leading the tournament over in England. The B.C.'s got Ty Tryon. Ty's just turned seventeen.

Family, media, and new friends surround him for twenty minutes after he finishes his round. "Think you can do it again tomorrow?" someone asks.

"Thank you," he replies. "Thank you very much." Then he goes out to the practice range and hits balls for two hours.

Ty Tryon has a blush of acne on his cheeks and a picture of Tiger Woods over his bed. Like Tiger, he had a personal trainer at age twelve and a sports psychologist at fifteen. Like Tiger, he and his dad hired IMG to be his agent. Like Howell, he plays Callaway, and again like Howell, he is taught by David Leadbetter. He turned pro this summer after finishing his sophomore year at Dr. Phillips High, a public school at home in Orlando. IMG quickly secured deals with Callaway for equipment and with Target for apparel that are worth about $1 million a year. In March, Tryon shot a ten-under-par 278 in the Honda Classic. His tie for thirty-ninth place was the best-ever finish on the PGA Tour for a sixteen-year-old. In December, Tryon would make it through all three stages of the PGA Tour qualifying tournament, a feat neither Woods nor Howell ever accomplished.

"In my opinion, it would have bordered on child abuse if we hadn't let him [turn pro]," Bill Tryon told Rick Reilly of *Sports Illustrated*. "Look, he's our son. We're going to work with him to help him in his chosen career. If that means not making him play at some charade of a golf college for two years to make everybody else feel better, so be it."

Surely Mr. Tryon was not referring to Stanford as the "charade of a golf college," although two years was exactly Tiger's tenure with the Cardinal. Yet Tiger's influence on this fundamental change in golf—as represented by Ty—could not be missed. *The New York Times*, May 5: "Tryon, 16, Leads a Youth Invasion in an Old Sport." *The Arizona Republic*, September 13: "Valley Boy taking aim at Tiger." Philip Francis, the Valley boy in the headline, is age twelve, five foot two, ninety-two pounds, and takes lessons from Jim Flick, Jack Nicklaus's instructor. He began entering tournaments at age four, has played in 190 events and won 102 of them, including seventeen of his last twenty-two.

The Orange County Register, August 1: "MINIATURE GOLF For 3-year-old, a hole-in-one is all in a day's play." Jake Paine, three foot two, thirty-five pounds, used a thirty-inch driver with a Snoopy head cover to ace the sixty-six-yard sixth hole at the Lake Forest Golf and Practice Club in Lake Forest, California. "It was a Tiger shot," Jake said. "I'm happy."

Tryon hits ball after ball at the practice range after his round, saluting Woods's dedication with his postround practice. A month before, in June, a flock of seventeen-year-old phenoms declared their allegiance in other ways. Many of the boys at the American Junior Golf Association Deloitte & Touche Junior Team Championship at Northwood Country Club in Dallas have assimilated every Tiger mannerism. They've got the right shoulder roll, the left-sleeve tug, and the cupped hands on either side of the bill of the hat, the better to focus while lining up a putt. The identification does not extend to clothing, however; none of them wear Nike, which they perceive to be more for muni course players. The fact that Polo is a major AJGA sponsor must also have something to do with it.

There's a kid popping a ball off the face of his driver with exquisite casualness while he waits to tee off—a variation of Tiger's hacky sack Nike commercial. Before each of his shots, the young man's father studies a scorecard and a yardage book and evaluates wind speed and direction with thrown blades of grass, as if he, not his kid, were about to hit the shot. Is he imitating Earl? You try to match the child with the parent, looking for similar mouths or chins or long legs. But differences seem less significant than sameness, because an identical air of intensity unites the mothers and fathers and sons and daughters.

"With the dawn of Tiger, this all changed," says Nancy Freeman Barragan, who, with her husband, Jim, founded this event. Their son Culley had a long, successful career as a junior golfer. "It's more macho. You have to work out. And the parents have become much more aggressive. Well, I found out a long time ago it didn't do any good to slap my leg when he missed a putt—kids are so in tune with your body language."

The game drew close three generations of Barragans and Freemans, but golf was still a nerd sport when their son started at age seven. "Now, all my friends think it's the coolest thing ever," says Culley Barragan, twenty-one, a senior member of the University of Texas golf team and a finalist to become a Rhodes Scholar. "Not just from the way Tiger looks and dresses but from the way golfers conduct themselves."

Little Culley was no piker—he took lessons from Randy Smith, who taught Justin Leonard—but he's sure he had more fun than the golfers he's watching today. "I don't know who changed first—the kids or their parents," he says. "Now they're so much more serious. We used to flirt with the girls in the tournament, and go to dinner or the movies with them. We'd wear costumes sometimes, like a dress shirt and a tie. I guess they see how much money there is in golf. It's like tennis was in the eighties."

Until Tiger, no one challenged the idea that the prime of a golfer's life occurred in his third, even his fourth decade. Just look at Hogan, who couldn't get arrested until he was thirty, and at Jack Nicklaus, who had probably his best year at age thirty-two, and won the Masters at forty-six. Now consider Tiger, a winner on the tour at twenty, and a big winner at twenty-one. Tiger begat Howell, Tryon, that twelve-year-old in Scottsdale, and the three-year-old with the Snoopy head cover in California.

"Tiger's taken a gentleman's game and turned it into a *sport,*" says Brandel Chamblee. "He's reduced the amount of time you need to be in it to become a champion. I think it's a permanent change. We all used to think that when you got to be forty, you'd have the same physical skills as when you were twenty, plus you'd be much smarter. Now the most important things seem to be reflexes and strength.

"Hal Sutton might punch me for saying this, because he can pick the bark off either side of a tree. But he can't beat Tiger, not consistently. Tiger's accurate, too, and he can hit driver 340 and two iron 250. He and Hal are just two different animals."

Back at the Deloitte & Touche Junior Team Championship, college coaches eye the best players and are surreptitiously eyed back by golfers and their parents. Is it a courtship between Mike Holder of Oklahoma State and Matt Rosenfeld, or a mere flirtation? And if they marry, will it last the full four years? Tiger proved you can get by very nicely with just two.

And at the B.C. Open, Ty Tryon accelerates the trend. The best golfers in the world are stronger, richer, less educated, and above all, younger. No one wants to wait to chase Tiger.

6

TIGERWOODSISGOD.COM

> It's just a job. Grass grows, birds fly, waves pound the sand. I beat people up.
>
> —Muhammad Ali

Oprah's all giddy.

"I'm feelin' y'all, I'm feelin' y'all," she says as her October 6 show begins, her voice reverting to her Mississippi roots. She was born in 1954 in tiny Kosciusko, dead in the rural heart of the state, an hour's drive from Yazoo City. But Oprah Winfrey, one of America's greatest capitalists and most admired women, proves every day that geography is not destiny.

She comments that there are far more men than usual in her studio in Chicago today. "I know you're here to see me—right," she says, then, in a voice like butter on grits: "You're here to see my son. My son has come home, and I'm so happy he's here." The producer shows us reaction shots of the audience, each member of which seems absolutely delighted to be with Oprah and her guest, who's just seconds from his entrance.

Using standard diction, she narrates a short video clip. "With his great passion and impeccable style, he's done the unthinkable—he has made golf *cool.* His appeal goes way beyond sports. People who don't know the difference between a birdie and a bogey are glued to the screen when Tiger plays. Not only is he on track to be the sports world's first billionaire, he could do it by the time he's thirty . . ." A moment later, Tiger comes out from behind the curtain, sharp as the edge of a knife in a black suit, light blue shirt, and a tie the color of dull gold. He and Oprah embrace, and the audience rises to applaud. There's a lot of love in this room.

Tiger's got a book to push, and this is the best place in the world to do it. Miss Winfrey began Oprah's Book Club in 1996, and since then each of the forty-odd books she's endorsed on her afternoon talk show have become best-sellers. Oprah books routinely sell hundreds of thousands of copies, but even that wouldn't satisfy Warner Books, which has printed an incredible 1.5 million copies of *How I Play Golf.*

Tiger does the full hour of Oprah and it's a brilliant show. The author had been on Oprah's stage a few years before, with Earl. He's more relaxed this time, because he's older, more experienced with the conventions of Q and A, and he's alone. With Tiger seated between himself and Oprah, Earl had caused a pregnant pause by referring to his son as an Oreo. But this time there is no glitch. The hostess offers mostly thoughtful questions, Tiger responds succinctly, and the audience hangs on every word and waits to clap or laugh. And instead of Earl, this show's costar is former NBA forward Charles Barkley, the future governor of Alabama, who has taped an interview that is interspersed throughout the show. "He is the most humble celebrity I've ever met in my life," Barkley says. "If I was as good as him, you couldn't control me. I'd walk around with a bullhorn to let people know I was comin' around.

"He is cheap. What's the word white folks use? Frugal. He's very *frugal*.

"I give him a hard time about scuba diving. I said, 'Black people don't scuba dive. I don't know any black person other than you who scuba dives.' Then I realized that he's got a mixture [of races], a Cablinasian thing. 'Well, that's the white part of you that goes scuba diving.' " ("Cablinasian," an amalgamation of Caucasian, black, Indian, and Asian, is the word Tiger invented to describe his racial makeup.)

Tiger also shows he knows how to get a laugh. He confirms *Time* magazine's report that yes, he is a neat-freak, that he makes his bed even in hotel rooms, and irons shirts that have already been professionally cleaned and pressed. "Anal," he says, and the hostess and the audience crack up.

For someone who's interviewed as much as he is, it's hell to come up with something new to say or a new way of saying something old, but today Tiger is eloquent. "I love to compete," he says. "That's the essence of who I am. I just chose golf as my avenue."

Oprah allows Tiger to be the star of the show, but she

doesn't exactly defer. Like her guest, she works with a live audience twenty feet away and with the world watching via the TV camera's unblinking eye. She's as big as or bigger than Tiger in her way, works just as hard, and her last name is just as superfluous. Her life might even be a template for Tiger's someday. She's a conglomerate with a positive, uplifting agenda, with money pouring in and influence going out. The main components of her empire are a film production company, called Harpo; a cable TV network, Oxygen; a magazine, *O*, "a personal growth guide for the new century"; her own charities, including one called A Better Chance, which gives college scholarships to inner-city kids; and a professorship at the Kellogg School of Management at Northwestern University (she and her boyfriend Stedman Graham teach a class on leadership). She's got Emmy this and Oscar nomination that and roomsful of awards and honors. After each show, she talks with her audience for two or three hours over tea and cookies. Thus she makes fifty great new friends five days a week. They tell their friends how wonderful Oprah is, and they tell their friends, and pretty soon you've got a magazine, a cable network, a professorship, two thriving charities, and the highest-rated afternoon talk show.

After a teaser for tomorrow's *Oprah*—featuring the emotional story of two sisters reconciling after ten years of not speaking—the hostess and her guest, both beaming, say goodbye. And the TV audience heads for the bookstore.

Not so fast, warns Alan Shipnuck in *Sports Illustrated*. "A recent search on Amazon.com turned up seventy-one books about Tiger Woods but *How I Play Golf* is the only one with his byline," Shipnuck writes. "That is what makes this instructional tome so disappointing. Instead of giving us a banquet of fresh insights, all Woods gives us is the reheated servings from his monthly *Golf Digest* lessons." Furthermore, writes Shipnuck, "the writing is formal and stilted—actually a good thing, because it captures Woods's cautious speech patterns—and filled with cloying homilies and banal accounts of his career."

Instead of an expansion of his ghost-written instruction articles, what Shipnuck and many others wanted was another *Down the Fairway*, Bobby Jones's graceful and self-effacing autobiography, written when he was Tiger's age. At twenty-five, Jones had been on the world stage for a decade. He was at least Tiger's equal: He'd won the U.S. Open twice, the U.S. Amateur twice, and the British Open—as an amateur, he could not play in the PGA, and he and Cliff Roberts hadn't yet invented the Masters. In addition to being golf's best player, Jones may have been its best writer. "I have a distinct recollection of falling off the veranda," he wrote, "headfirst into a garbage can. It is lucky for me that I do not have to trust everything to memory, for I have no independent recollection of ever getting out of the can."

Jack Nicklaus was another of the rare athletic champions who paused in mid-career to look back at his life. Although *The Greatest Game of All* is too obviously the work of coauthor Herbert Warren Wind—"distance lends enchantment off the tee," Wind wrote, a phrasing Jack would never use in a million years—it's still a useful look at what Jack thought about himself and his game at age twenty-nine.

Not so *How I Play Golf,* which provides great instruction but no introspection. It succeeds very well, however, if you realize it's a thirty-five-dollar picture book, evolving not from corny golf instruction manuals or cowritten autobiography but from a completely different tradition, the photo-filled volumes providing peeks of Marilyn Monroe, Madonna, and Betty Page. The golf tips in *How I Play Golf,* in other words, are secondary to the crystal images of Tiger's starburst smile, his large, liquid, slightly hooded eyes, his track man's body, and the hypnotic power and grace of his golf swing. It's Tiger being Tiger, seen but not heard. It's a fan magazine between hard covers.

AND WHAT'S WRONG with a fan magazine? Ultimately, every component of the Tiger empire grows from the fertile earth of the masses of people who like him but will never meet him. They buy his books and the products he endorses, and they attend his tournaments, ask for his autograph, and support his charities. Or they don't. As we learned in high school, popularity is a fleeting thing, tied insecurely to an angel's wing. We'll love Tiger as long as he keeps winning and doesn't get arrested. When he stops being the best, who knows?

The suffix "mania" first attached to the proper noun "Tiger" when he turned pro in 1996. The wave crested when he won the 1997 Masters by twelve, and it hasn't come down much since. Magazine covers and sold-out tournaments hint at his status, and the tremendous spike in TV viewership when he is playing versus when he is not confirms it. But to really feel Tigermania, you must soldier on through his gallery and see what they see and hear what they say. It's a constantly reconvening group similar to the heyday of Arnie's Army thirty years ago, yet it's unlike any golf audience ever seen before.

In August, a month after Duval's talent overcame his history and he won his first major at the British Open, the PGA commences at the Atlanta Athletic Club. With its paved pond edges and its concrete cart paths, it's got a kind of perfection to it. Its sight lines are great and the walking is easy, which makes AAC the perfect place to watch Tiger.

Except that there's not enough room. Even on spacious courses like the TPC Las Colinas, Champions, and Atlanta Athletic Club, Tiger's fans' biggest problem is each other. So in a way, it's fortunate that they are the least knowledgeable spectators on the course. How could they be anything else, when their main (or only) connection to golf is this one man? While it's unfair to characterize a large collection of people by the actions of just a few, many more than just a few people elbow each other like power forwards to get a better look when Tiger hits a shot, and they sprint to the next vantage point after Tiger hits, and leave the green en masse after Tiger holes out. His fans salute Tiger's good shots, especially his birdie putts, with enthusiasm often out of all proportion to the accomplishment. All of this is rude, of course, and it bothers the other players. And it's exactly what used to happen in Arnie's gallery.

The situation is already getting better, however, as all the newcomers, black and white, young and old, get used to the golf etiquette deal. "I remember him saying at the orientation meeting [for those just joining the Tour], 'I'm gonna cause some problems and confusion,'" says Henry Hughes, chief of operations of the Tour's Championship Management. "He brought so many new fans with him, who just didn't know when to talk and when to stand. It was most evident at the Tour Championship in Tulsa in '97. I mean, full-length London Fog raincoats, and shoes that just *weren't right* for watching golf."

"Go Ti-GER!" "Go Ar-NIE!" While the exuberance and hooting of Palmer's gallery back in the day matches that of Tiger's fans today, there's one important difference. The object of affection back in 1965 needed the energy he felt from the throng outside the ropes. In the phrase back then, he "fed off" their enthusiasm. You couldn't walk along with the army and not feel the circularity of the thing, that the more excited the crowd was the more birdies Arnold would make, and the more birdies Arnold made the more excited the walking, skipping, running gallery would become. Tiger's vibe is different. Self-sufficient and self-motivating, he cannot interact with his fans and still concentrate. His celebratory uppercuts not withstanding, he comports himself more like Hogan than like Palmer. And when he's not playing well, there's none of that steely, jaw-setting "I'm not done yet" manner Arnie had. "When Tiger's not winning, he always looks like he's about to cry," comments a fifteen-year-old golfer in Texas.

But he doesn't, even when he has cause to. At the Tour Championship in Houston in November, the last significant tournament of the year, someone in the fitness van rubs Tiger the wrong way before the first round, and he plays with stabbing pain in his back all day. Walking all eighteen holes with him inside the ropes yields several vivid impressions, and first among them is that he is what he says he is, a competitor. It's muggy and overcast, and a brewing storm in the Gulf gives the day a sense of unease that mirrors Tiger's mood. The knot in his lumbar spine causes him to wince on his follow-through and makes an ordeal of picking up his tee from the ground or his ball from the hole. But Tiger will not confirm the obvious for roving TV reporter Judy Rankin, that his back is just killing him. He marches stoically along, and an equilateral triangle of sweat appears on his tan shirt over the small of his back. Finally he comes to a complete halt on the eleventh hole. After hitting his three-wood tee shot, he takes twenty steps down the fairway, stops, and bends deeply from the waist. Seven security guards stop with him, encircling him, looking outward, and scanning the crowd at this moment when their protectee seems so vulnerable.

He shoots 70 despite the pain.

"He's kind of majestic, an awesome presence," whispers a woman seeing Tiger for the first time. The shadow of a jet ripples over the golf course and the six-deep human fence surrounding the ninth green. "He's like royalty. You notice entire families out here. But it's really a chase to be in his gallery."

Up close, Tiger's no-ass, fat-free body overlaid with muscle brings to mind a hummingbird that's spent a lot of time in the gym. His fitness and the fitness he's inspired in the other top golfers serves to widen the gulf between him and the softies who watch him and write about him. Up close, you see what a bad idea his chin whiskers are: This wispy beginning of a goatee somehow makes his skull look small. (Thus his year is bookended with bad hair decisions, since he began the year with a blond dye job that made him look like a pop singer.) And inside the ropes, you get a hint of the goldfish bowl feeling he lives with all the time. You also get a better view, of course, which several fans vocally resent. “That’s bullshit,” a young man with a tattoo on his neck says loudly. “How come he gets to walk in there?”

In Atlanta, Tiger’s troops wear Nike, which is not unusual, but they address him between shots like he’s playing basketball, which is: “Come on, Tiger, let’s go, let’s go,” one man says, repeating phrases as a basketball coach must. “Here we go, Tiger,” says another man when Woods walks by on the fourteenth fairway. “Here we go, here we go, here we go.” He claps his hands to punctuate his message, which seems to be: Let’s see a little more *hustle* out there!

Lots of pierced, tattooed white kids always follow Woods. That is, white *boys*: his gallery seems more male than you might expect. Palmer attracted far more women. According to National Golf Foundation numbers, 676,000 black people in the United States declared themselves to be golfers in 1996. Three years later, the number had swelled to 882,000, and no one wonders why. Yet of the tournaments in Augusta, Irving, Columbus, Tulsa, Atlanta, and Houston in 2001, only Tiger’s northern Georgia gallery seems much racially mixed.

“We try to be like Tiger,” says Philis Johnson, seventeen, watching the slow-moving theater on the practice tee at the Tour Championship. “I have his poster up in my room, the one where he's crouching down, lining up a putt? I started to play golf in May '97. My girlfriend called when the Masters was on TV and she said, '*Man*, did you see him? He's cute, right?' I had a golf lesson right after Mother's Day." Her mother stands in the background, beaming at the enthusiasm and beauty of her daughter, a daughter who remembers Mother's Day. Philis is on the golf team at Lamar High in Houston, has an A average, and she's trying to make the Tiger Woods Foundation team.

But she's got no swooshes. "I'm Wal-Mart!" Philis says with a laugh. Her friend, Clarence Preston, sixteen, smiles shyly as he searches his person for Nike logos to prove his loyalty to Tiger. He finds two on his $140 white patent leather shoes. He locates a third when he lifts his outer garment to reveal an inner undershirt that reads CYNERGY HOUSTON JUNIOR GOLF I AM TIGER WOODS. Clarence is the number-one man on the high-school golf team at Alief Hastings, a western suburb. He also aspires to make the Tiger Woods Foundation squad. Philis and Clarence are lovable kids who love Tiger.

Willie Evans and Ben Cooksey look bemused at the spectacle of their young friends being interviewed. Evans, seventy-one, a former caddie, wears a hat advertising the Forever Young Leisure and Social Club. Apropos of nothing much, he tells a Doug Sanders story, about the time the colorful pro saw him at a golf course wearing one black shoe and one brown and said, "Where'd you get them shoes at? I gotta get me a pair of those." So Sanders went into the golf shop and bought Willie his first pair of golf shoes.

Cooksey, fifty-seven, a patch of white chest hair peeking out of the top of his striped golf shirt, seems impatient with Willie's digression. "I'll tell you what Tiger's done," he says. "He gets a seventy-year-old black woman calling me on the phone whenever he's in a tournament. 'How's Tiger doin'? How's Tiger doin'?' She don't care about golf. She just cares about Tiger.

"These kids today don't have a chance," he says. "If the world don't gobble them up, the other kids will. But this [he gestures toward Tiger on the practice tee and the throng watching him] can happen to her or to him [he points to Philis and Clarence]. The whole thing is attitude. It can get you anything you want or it can stop you dead. And you need something to believe in. Like Tiger has his mother's Budi-ism."

Religious thoughts often occur to the true Tiger believer. "The chosen one," said the truest believer, Earl Woods. "He'll have the power to move nations." *Sports Illustrated* writer Gary Smith "bought in," as they say: He titled his essay about Tiger "The Messiah." "No, no, no," says Pete McDaniel, a *Golf Digest* writer and coauthor of two Tiger Woods books, *Training a Tiger* and *How I Play Golf.* McDaniel, a strong Christian, has begun a golf ministry to blend his two passions. "Tiger is not a god and he is not a prophet. But I believe God picks special people to do special things. And I believe God sent Tiger here on a special mission: to bring people together. I've already seen it happening around the world, people standing shoulder to shoulder just to get a look at him."

John Ziegler was unusually receptive to the imagery Earl

suggested. Ziegler is a thirty-four-year-old talk radio host without portfolio but with a zero handicap and a sense of humor. He attended Georgetown, the great Jesuit university, but after college he found himself losing his religion. During the Masters in 2000—on April 1—he declared himself the pastor of the First Church of Tiger Woods and launched a Web site called tigerwoodsisgod.com. "Tiger made no effort to deny his divinity, by the way," Ziegler says. "And his lawyers made no effort to get in touch."

Although the Church stretches past good taste, as a publicity vehicle, it was genius. Since launching the site, Ziegler spends most mornings of major tournaments talking to sports and talk radio stations around the country. He has appeared on MSNBC and the BBC, and in the pages of the *New York Times, Sports Illustrated* and *Der Spiegel.* In its story, *Maximum Golf* predictably played it to the hilt, putting Ziegler in a priest's clothes with burning candles and stained glass in the background. He loves it: The pastor of the First Church of Tiger Woods is a showman, with a great voice and an easy way with words. "On MSNBC, I said that Tiger's win in the 2000 U.S. Open was the greatest human achievement since Lindbergh flew across the Atlantic alone," Ziegler says. "That got a few laughs."

The big question, of course, is what percentage of this is tongue in cheek, and what amount, if any, is serious? "My goal was to thread the needle, so that those who think this is real can believe it, and those that want to take it as a joke can do that, too," Ziegler says. "Click on the testimonials section on the Web site. It's fascinating. Half the people think I'm doomed to hell and half totally get it."

So which is it? Ziegler straddles the fence. While the First Church of Tiger Woods is completely fictitious, there is, he says, "a serious side to this. Tiger's on the verge of perfecting a human endeavor that has never been perfected before, and there's something godlike in that. He never lets you down. He's something to believe in."

TIGER DOES NOT WIN the PGA at Atlanta in August—David Toms does, with Mickelson second. TIGER'S LOST SUMMER banners a golf magazine. We should all be so lost. Later in the month he wins the one-million-dollar first prize at the World Golf Championships/Nippon Electronics Corporation Invitational. At the end of the year, he'll have won the Masters plus four other tournaments on the U.S. Tour—more than anyone—and $5.6 million, also more than anyone else. Including all tournament prize money, Tiger will win $7.7 million, two million more than the runner-up, Sergio Garcia. But if Tiger's 2001 was falling short of the glory of his 2000, that could easily be fixed in one long weekend at the end of September. At the Belfry, in England. At the Ryder Cup.

But violent idiots crashed planes into buildings and called it religion, and golf and golfers faded from view and from importance. Woods got the horrible news during a practice round for the World Golf Championship/American Express Championship in St. Louis. With flights grounded, he rented a car and drove home to Florida. And with only weeks between September 11 and the start of the big biennial match, the Ryder Cup was quickly postponed for a year. Some of those with the energy to worry about it blamed the postponement on Tiger. At this time of deep national melancholy, their thinking went, we needed a circus and we needed to show the world our disdain for the terrorists—and we'd have both if Tiger wanted it. But Ryder Cup captain Curtis Strange and other credible men in the thick of the decision snorted at the idea that Tiger had the power to decide the fate of the match. As far as we knew, Woods was the only pro inspiring the lunatic fringe to phone in death threats when he played in golf tournaments—so asking him to do more than he already does seemed both dishonest and too easy. Unless, of course, he actually wanted the leadership role his father obviously had in mind for him.

"Someday, with his recognition and status in golf he'll be able to effect changes because most of the world leaders are golfers," Earl told *Golfweek* shortly before September 11. "He can go in and say, "Hey, Muhammad, how's your game? Want a lesson? And by the way, those prisoners you've got, give them to me. I'm taking them back. And those kids you've got, they need food.' And they'll say, 'We'll take care of it, Mr.Woods.' "

Earl's interesting ideas about diplomacy begged the question of whether Tiger is now, or will ever be, interested in that sort of thing. "Every time he has been presented with a chance to make a social comment, he has turned and walked the other way," wrote Christine Brennan in *USA Today* during U.S. Open week. "He's all Jordan and Griffey and O'Meara, all about corporate acquiescence and playing it safe on the sponsor's dime." True enough—Tiger risked no opinion on causes celebres such as his Stanford teammate Casey Martin or the Confederate flag. Of course, he could get away with his safe silence a lot more easily if his father suddenly lost his voice, and if people stopped comparing him to pioneers like Arthur Ashe and Jackie Robinson. But why should Tiger speak for himself, when Nike and the others paid him so much to speak for them?

"He's exceeded everyone's expectations on the golf course, but in terms of social contributions, he's disappointing," said a well-connected journalist who requested anonymity. "Tiger has established this pattern of insularity. He follows his friend Michael Jordan, who disappeared on the Nike sweatshop issue. Has Tiger *ever* taken a stand? He gets a pass because four days a year he does a clinic for the Tiger Woods Foundation and his time's worth a lot. But what we miss is his voice. We don't know what he thinks. Or if he thinks.

"Compare him to Muhammad Ali at the same age. Right or wrong, whether or not his hand was forced, whether he was manipulated or not, Ali stood for something. And he never hid. He was vilified and exiled but he still walked by himself through Central Park. Michael Jordan and Tiger Woods are the direct opposite of that."

Howell was in the air en route to Tampa when the planes crashed. When his own flight was grounded in New Orleans, he and fellow Tour players Chris Tidland and Willie Wood rented a van and drove to Florida. When the Tampa Bay Classic Presented by Buick was canceled, he rented another vehicle and drove home to Oklahoma.

Before the first round of the first tournament after 9/11, the Marconi Pennsylvania Classic, Howell took a half-hour drive into the country to visit the crater caused by the crash of one of the hijacked planes. United Flight 93 may have been intended to destroy the White House but was brought down in an isolated area south of the old steel mill town of Johnstown by some very brave passengers. Howell stood silently for a few minutes, awed by the size of the hole and by what it meant.

At the next event, The Texas Open at La Cantera in San Antonio, professional golf expressed itself regarding the terrorist attacks. An amusement park called Six Flags Fiesta Texas sprawled adjacent to La Cantera, and it had an outdoor amphitheater perfect for the occasion. In a bus for the short ride from the golf course to the park, a caddie examined the flier for the program called A Tribute to America. "Not freaking Lee Greenwood again," he said. Greenwood's a country singer with pipes like a cathedral organ and a patriotic song called "I'm Proud to Be an American." "Every time there's a war, he has another hit. Where would his career be without the occasional war?" But that was the last bit of cynicism on this warm September night.

A huge American flag dominated the rear of the stage but a little gold cup on a royal blue cube in front of the podium caught the eye—the Ryder Cup. In blue blazer, red tie, and khaki pants, the team's captain entered from stage right. "As I spoke with the team members," said Curtis Strange, his voice thickening, "all of them were full of emotion and disbelief. All of them wanted to be home with their families." This was to have been Ryder Cup week, and this rally was supposed to have been the U.S. Ryder Cup team's show of unity against the terrorists. But besides Captain Curtis, only David Toms, Hal Sutton, Scott Hoch, and Jesper Parnevik (from the European side) showed up.

Strange announced a $520,000 donation to the September 11 Relief Fund from the Ryder Cup players. Jack Connelly, on behalf of the PGA of America—the club professionals organization—pledged another half million. The PGA Tour and the Golf Course Owners Association promised millions more. The Trinity Baptist Church Chorale sang with flags sewn on the chests of their red choir robes, the Air Force Band of the West played "America the Beautiful," and Greenwood sang with the veins in his neck standing out from the effort like subcutaneous snakes. Square-jawed tough guy Hal Sutton wore a gray suit and choked up when he spoke, and most of the thousands present choked up with him. "I hope this feeling of unity spreads throughout the world," Parnevik said, "and lasts until well after this war."

Unity, death, heroism—the rally inspired thoughts on some big ideas. Especially heroism. Would September 11 begin or accelerate the death knell of the modern athletic hero? Even the ancient Greeks, who erected bronze and stone statues of their athletic champions, eventually grew tired of the mere musclemen. "Of all the countless evils throughout Hellas, none is worse than the race of athletes," wrote Euripedes in the fifth century B.C. "In youth, they strut about in splendor, the idols of the city . . . [but] who ever helped his fatherland by winning a crown for wrestling, or for speed of foot, or hurling the diskos, or striking a good blow on the jaw?"

The answer, Mr. Euripedes, is that twenty-six centuries later, great athletes do help the commonweal. Because a lot of the world is addicted to entertaining itself. Take film-music-sports-TV from a typical twenty-five-year-old American male's life and there won't be much left but his job and the Taco Bell wrappers on the floor. Yet for reasons cultural, sociological, and public relational, the biggest games are losing their grip. The analysis is easy: All you have to do is look at TV ratings. In 2000, compared to 1996, the NBA was down 34 percent. The NFL was off 6 percent. Major League Baseball lost 4 percent of its viewers, and NASCAR was flat. Golf—"television's hottest sport" according to *Golf World*, which supplied these numbers—increased its watchers by 7 percent. And thank you, Tiger.

But professional golf, with so much of its popularity tied up in one man, looks a lot like the NBA before the fall—that is, before the retirement of Michael Jordan. Tiger's vulnerability, and thus golf's danger, is that he will be seen as cynical and uncaring, as overexposed as the Nike logo, and tight with a buck and with gratitude despite his wealth. And TV sports may be threatened again by the sea change of September 11, which reminded us that none of the players are heroes. After all, what really was the bravery of making a five-foot putt for a million dollars compared to running up the stairs of a burning building on a civil servant's pay? How could we ever again bear to listen to a multimillionaire golf pro bitch about bumpy greens or early starting times or the length of his private jet trip or someone using his picture without adequate compensation when men his own age were fighting and dying in a foreign war?

Crazes come and go, and mega-events stop and start them. In an instant, Tiger went from the most popular and visible American to someone well down the list behind Bush and Giuliani and the other heroes of 9/11.

TIGERMANIA COULD REEMERGE if Woods can get what Ali had in Frazier, what Hogan had in Nelson and Snead, what Palmer had in Nicklaus and Nicklaus had in Watson. A Woods-and-somebody rivalry could invigorate the top of the sport for years to come and trickle down to the rest of us.

In the back of a black limousine following Ben Hogan's hearse, Sam Snead discussed his great success when competing head-to-head against his recently deceased nemesis. Years before, Hogan had denigrated Snead's intellect and questioned Nelson's dedication. Nelson wondered about the mental makeup of a man—Hogan—who lived on the road but hated strangers, and who seemed to prefer a fight over getting along. "I can beat the fat kid on his best day," Arnold Palmer said at the dawn of his publicly polite war against Jack. He sometimes excused himself from the table by saying he had to "go take a Nicklaus." A delicious component of their battle was that it spilled over to their fans. The Army in Augusta was so rabidly anti-Jack in the early sixties that Bobby Jones felt compelled to write a brief essay on golf course comportment that is still printed on the back of a Masters ticket. "Most distressing to those who love the game of golf is the applauding or cheering of misplays or misfortune of a player . . ." And when Jack got a shirt deal and his own logo, Arnie's infantrymen would observe the Golden Bear on the cloth above someone's heart and ask, "How come you've got a pig on your shirt?"

Someday one of the young guns like Charles Howell may beat Tiger often enough and at the right times to establish a long-running battle. Of the guys in his immediate wake, Duval is too emotionally remote and too much Tiger's friend to give their give-and-take an edge, and Garcia is too bubbly for the opposing team to dislike. A Mickelson-Woods feud might be just the ticket. While Tiger is frugal, Phil enjoys paying the kid at the lemonade stand with a folded and refolded bill and telling him to keep the change, just to watch the youngster's face when he realizes it's a hundred. Tiger dates, Phil mates; Mickelson's home life is such a big deal to him that he took a four-month vacation at the end of 2001. While no one claims there's any personal enmity between the two, and their list of similarities is longer than a list of their differences, they are not friends.

But until it's Phil or David or Sergio or Charles beating Tiger by one at the Masters instead of the other way around, the real Woods rivalry will remain his intriguing pursuit of the ghost of Jack Nicklaus. Jack won eighteen majors, the most ever. Tiger has won six. Tiger wants to beat Jack's record, which would be more or less objective proof that he would be the new best golfer ever. But major measurement is an indication, not a definition. Wars, injuries—even disagreement about what constitutes a "major" tournament—all this makes historical comparisons as difficult in golf as in any other sport. Thus the Nicklaus-Woods rivalry is complex and psychological, with Tiger as Ahab and Jack as the white whale. Many redwoods will have to die to provide the paper on which to write the gradually revealed story of Tiger chasing Jack.

Tiger at twenty-five was a little ahead of Jack at the same age in some things and a little behind in others. Jack led in kids, three to zero, and wives, one to nothing. Tiger led in majors, six to four; in PGA Tour events won, twenty-nine to seventeen; and in aircraft. In July 1964, when Jack was twenty-four, he bought the hot new Aero Commander 680 FL, a twin-engine prop plane with a cruising speed of 220 MPH at ten thousand feet and a thousand-mile range. Tiger's got him there—the jets he uses fly close to two or three times as fast, five times as high, and clear across the United States without refueling.

Both were with IMG, but Tiger made a ton more money because tons more were available from the global companies he endorsed. Jack had a rivalry that brought out his best and sharpened interest in the game, but he was the black hat compared to Arnie. Tiger has no close rival and is far more loved than Jack was at the same age (Nicklaus, it should be pointed out, had a midcareer fashion and image makeover—more hair, less weight, better clothes—that helped make him almost as popular as Palmer). Both Jack and Tiger absolutely crushed the ball, and crushed it straight. In Jack's famous third-round 64 in the '65

Masters, he hit wedges to four par 4s on the front nine, a three iron onto the par 5 eighth, and five irons onto the surface on the two par 5s on the back. This in a relatively dead-ball era, with wooden woods and steel shafts. At age twenty-five, Jack's best years still lay ahead. Tiger may have peaked in 2000 when he won nine tournaments including three majors. But at whatever moment they were at their best, who would beat who?

"I'd have to take Jack," Lee Trevino told *Golf Digest*. "He was longer than Tiger for one thing, and a better putter. He'd game-plan Tiger to death. Nicklaus at his best always found a way to win."

Sam Snead would pick—Sam Snead. "People ask me if I could have beaten Tiger Woods in my prime. Well, hell yes, I could have. In my prime I could do anything with a golf ball I wanted, and no man scared me on the golf course."

Tom Weiskopf would take Nicklaus if the weapons were persimmon and balata and Woods if both had to play modern equipment. But in this time machine duel that will never take place, with both men at the peak of their skills, Weiskopf likes Tiger "because he's a better athlete than Jack."

In terms of years at the top, Nicklaus was the North Star. Jack reigned from 1964 until 1976, perhaps a little longer. That's about double the heavyweight championship terms of Nelson, Hogan, Palmer, and Watson. Tiger will need to sustain his excellence over a long period of time to reach Jack's heights. So the richer food for thought than a comparison of the Bear and the Tiger at age twenty-five is: What will Eldrick T. Woods be doing at age fifty, and what will he have done?

"He will have broken every golf record imaginable, by a wide margin," says writer Pete McDaniel. "Because of him, you'll see that at least 20 percent of the fields of all the events on all the tours will be minorities, and he'll relish the fact that he brought them together. His impact will be far-ranging.

"And I think he'll be doing just what Earl did at fifty—he'll be training his own little Tiger."

Guy Yocom, McDaniel's colleague at *Golf Digest* and the other actual author of *How I Play Golf*, foresees a more sedentary couch-based Tiger on the day his AARP card arrives. "People don't appreciate how hard he works and how fast he's going," Yocom says. "Between the things he does in business, and golf, and the fans just crushing him, and his security, which is a real issue—burnout is a real possibility. He's won six majors—eighteen's a million miles away. I don't think he'll make it."

A number of respondents expect public office for Tiger, this multiethnic man who might unite the races. Earl speaks vaguely about him being an ambassador-at-large, sort of Jesse Jackson with a golf club. Perhaps Woods Senior pictures something even bigger, another Akbar the Great, the philosopher-king who united India in the sixteenth century. A Moslem, "He had a flair for humoring all the creeds," wrote Will Durant in *The Story of Civilization*. Sometimes Akbar wore in public a Hindu bindi (a mark on his forehead) or a Zoroastrian sacred shirt. When some Jesuits came to Delhi, Akbar allowed them free rein to go after converts, and he had his scribes translate the New Testament. "While Catholics were murdering Protestants in France," writes

Durant, "and Protestants were murdering Catholics in England, and the Inquisition was killing and robbing Jews in Italy, Akbar invited all the representatives of all the religions in his empire to a conference, pledged them to peace, issued edicts of toleration for every cult and creed, and, as evidence of his own neutrality, married wives from the Brahman, Buddhist, and Mohammedan faiths."

John Ziegler, the tigerwoodsisgod.com guy, notes that "Tiger will be eligible to run for president in 2012. He'd be perfect electorally, since he grew up in California and lives in Florida. Oprah could be his running mate."

One respondent mentioned the UN ambassadorship for the fifty-year-old Tiger, another the presidency of Thailand, his mother's native country. Bangkok needs cleaning up. Preposterous, says a writer with a national publication. "I hear people talk about him going into politics. With what? I don't think he reads a goddamn newspaper, much less a book. I think he's a *golfer.*" The reporter did not want to be named, because "Tiger loathes writers and he's vindictive, and I can't afford to get cut off."

Brett Avery, editor, *Golf Journal*, the USGA magazine: "I'll be disappointed if he's still playing golf at age 50."

Jim Frank, editor, *Golf Magazine*: "I think he'll be like Greg Norman—burned out and fed up. He'll have won twenty-five to thirty majors. But something's going to have to change to keep him interested. Will the new young guns be enough?"

Byron Nelson: "I think he'll continue to do a lot with children. He's good at it. And there's hardly a better thing anyone could do."

Lance Barrow, CBS Sports: "I think he'll be doing exactly what he said he'll be doing. He'll have his bag on the back of a cart on the Senior Tour and Steve Williams will be driving the cart."

Larry Nelson, Senior PGA Tour: "He'll have a business empire, potentially, like Greg Norman. I can't picture him at thirty-five or thirty-eight still having the desire to compete."

Brandel Chamblee, PGA Tour: "Historically, no one at his level ever completely quits golf. But I don't see him on the Senior Tour, or designing courses. I think he'll be involved in a worldwide charity, something with his name on it. He has the only thing that's better than being lucky—he knows he's lucky. Whatever he does, it will be on his own terms. He will transcend golf."

Maybe he won't do anything to keep our attention and admiration. For no one in this life is required to lead the race every day, every year, no matter what his daddy says. Some picture Tiger at two score and ten losing the battle of middle-age spread, his increasingly Earl-like body parked in a courtside seat at Los Angeles Lakers games next to the 2024 equivalents of Jack Nicholson and Dyan Cannon.

BACK IN AUSTIN, the faux Tiger continues to hit balls, pump his fist, hit balls. But his portrayal took a severe beating in a recent U.S. Open qualifier, which is unwise to enter armed only with swooshes and sincerity instead of actual skill. He shot 105. The USGA sent a letter disinviting him from the competition until such time as he could demonstrate that he really could play the game.

Hope, fantasy, and the delusion of a million wanna-bes trot behind Tiger, who is himself running a race. Some of his opponents are as invisible and ethereal as history and expectations, but he feels the breath of living foes, too—the annoying press, the insatiable fans, fast-closing thoroughbreds named Duval, Mickelson, and Garcia, and waves of new sprinters represented by Howell and Tryon. In one way or another, all of them want what Tiger has: his game, his fame, his attention, or his autograph.

There's glory in the chase for the strivers with clubs in their hands and sweat on their arms. But for the rest of us there's the realization that we may never catch Eldrick T. Woods. He's lapped the field and snuck up from behind. He's calling the shots, as tigers always do.

POSTSCRIPT

Charles Howell won $1.5 million and was named PGA Tour Rookie of the Year for 2001. He also fired his caddie and his agent.

Rocky Hambric, Howell's agent, sued.

IMG got two important new clients: Jack Nicklaus and Charles Howell III.

Tiger Woods won $5.6 million and the Vardon Trophy for lowest stroke average, and was named Player of the Year for the fourth time by the Golf Writers Association of America.

A private campaign has begun to raise $1.5 million for the survivors of Tulsa's 1921 race riot. The money will be used for a museum, a memorial, scholarships, and $5,000 payments, too.

In late July, News Corporation put *Maximum Golf* up for sale. There were no takers for the Tiger-inspired publication, and it folded.

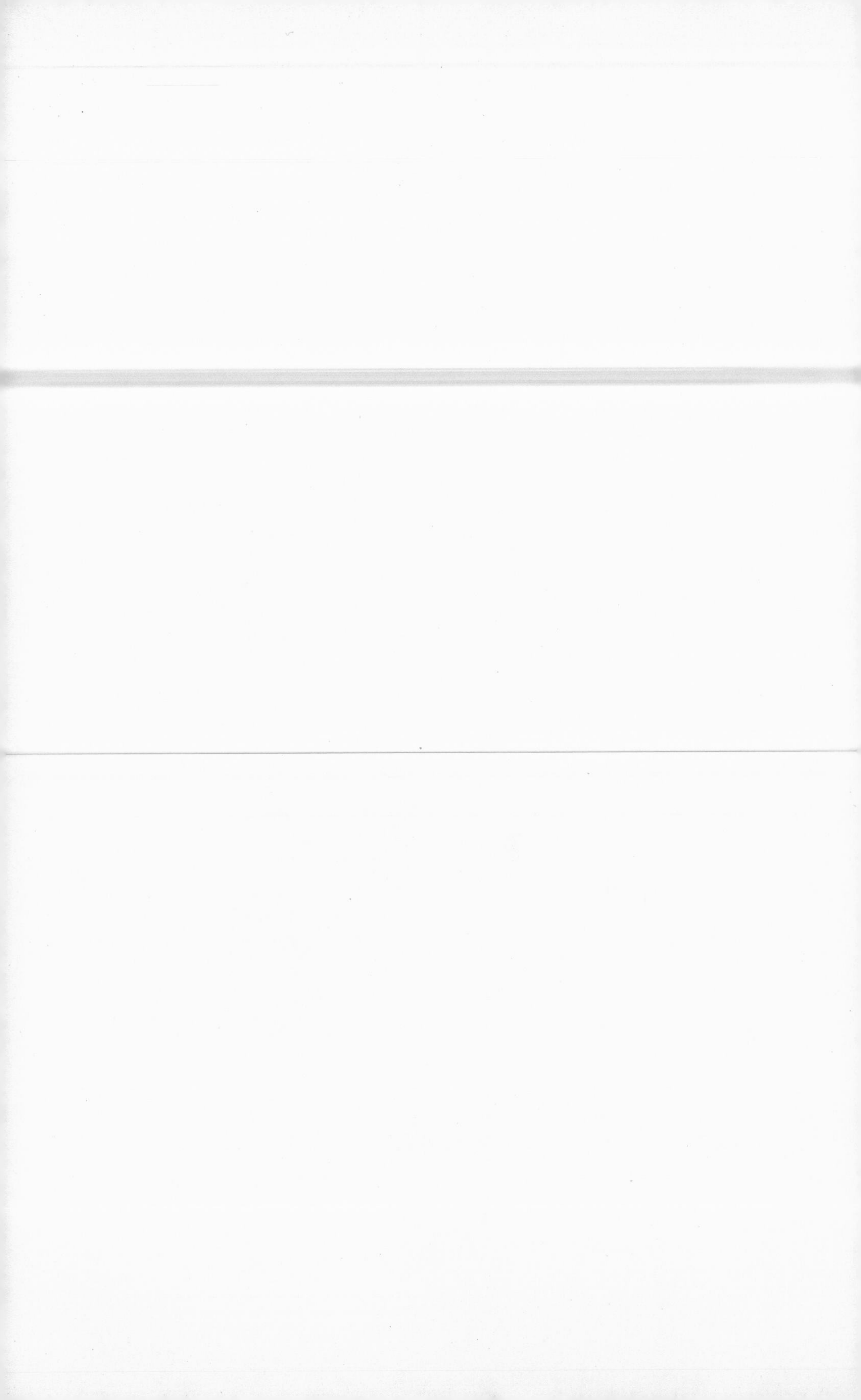